MB

Amaro
MONTENEGRO
LUXARDO
MARASCHINO
CHERRIES
CASAMIGOS
Tequila
Jalisco, Mexico
BOMBAY
NEGRONI
LEMON DROP
MARTINI
DIRTY MARTINI
EXTRA DRY
VERMOUTH

HAPPY HOUR AT HOME

100 RECIPES FOR SNACKING AND SIPPING WITH FRIENDS

ELIZABETH VAN LIERDE

Photography by Abagail Halstead

weldon**owen**

UDSEN FAMILY
ORGANIC
just
neapple
00% PINEAPPLE JUICE
FROM CONCENTRATE
SPICY TAMA
GM
SERVE CHILLED
EL ÚNIC
GRA
MA
LIQUEU
Fre

For my mom, for showing me that
making people feel welcome is an art form.

Contents

HENDRICK'S
MIDSUMMER SOLSTICE
HENDRICK'S
GIN
AMASS
DRY GIN
BEEFEATER
LONDON
LONDON DRY GIN
MALFY
GIN
ORIGINALE
ITALY
AVIATION
AMERICAN GIN
BATCH DISTILLED
LEOPOLD'S
EMPRESS
INDIGO GIN
Tanqueray
LONDON DRY GIN
CAMPARI
MILANO
Pumpkin
Spice
CANE RU
RUM
GRAY
WHALE
GIN

INTRODUCTION

HELLOOO! COME ON IN!

Hi there. I'm so happy you're here. If we were meeting face-to-face, I would be handing you a La Dolce Vita Margarita (page 43) and asking how life has been treating you. And that's exactly the laid-back vibe I want you to feel while flipping through this book. Take off your coat and find a comfy spot. You're in for a treat.

If you're new here, welcome. I'm thrilled that you picked up this book (truly, thank you!). I know you'll love it. And if you have been here since my first book, *Everyday Entertaining*, welcome back! I can't wait to share this next chapter of the story with you.

This time around, I'm bringing you *Happy Hour at Home*, my collection of recipes celebrating the joy of hosting friends and family at home without the pressure of perfection and performance.

I'M GOING TO TAKE A WILD GUESS THAT YOU ENJOY ENTERTAINING, ARE ALWAYS DOWN FOR HAPPY HOUR, AND LOVE SPLITTING A BOTTLE OF ICE-COLD SAUV BLANC WITH YOUR FRIENDS AS MUCH AS I DO. IF THAT SOUNDS LIKE YOU, YOU'RE IN THE RIGHT PLACE.

Since writing my first book, life has been a bit of a roller coaster (for real).

A few years ago, my partner and I went on an unforgettable and inspiring trip to Italy, where we indulged in the Italian custom of the apericena. That meant starting every evening meal with a spritz, small plates of salty snacks and appetizers, and long, lingering conversations. Sometimes the spread was so bountiful and the conversation so engrossing that our apericena became our dinner.

Soon after that glorious Italian getaway, I turned thirty, and in a devastating turn, I lost my mom to cancer. (See what I mean by roller coaster?) In 2024, I sort of hit the reset button on life.

I cried a lot, took a vacation to Hawaii, refocused my career, cooked comfort food, drank a lot of wine, and moved into a new home—a home that I affectionately nicknamed Hotel Rascal, after our dog. Our home became a foundation for new inspiration for what I love: a place to gather, celebrate, and make memories.

Somewhere between grieving and long afternoons on the patio, I entered what I call my "happy hour of life."

CAN I TELL YOU A SECRET?

For the last couple of years or so, I've been dreaming of opening my own bar—Bar Elizabeth. There, I've said it. My second La Dolce Vita Marg must be kicking in, ha! If you're ready for a snack, I can make us some Whipped Feta Dip with Spicy Citrus Olives (page 20).

There is something about saying what you want out loud that makes a dream way more real, isn't there? I bet you're thinking about one of your dreams now too.

But I don't think running a restaurant is for me. I've seen *The Bear*, and I know my cortisol levels couldn't hang. That meant I had no choice but to switch up my plan. Writing a cookbook of incredibly tasty cocktails and satisfying snacks fulfilled my Bar Elizabeth dream.

SO INSTEAD OF CREATING A BAR IN THE NEIGHBORHOOD, I HAVE MADE ONE FOR YOU RIGHT AT HOME.

In this book, I share my collection of easy yet memorable beverages and light bites inspired by iconic happy hours that you can make for your own happy hour at home. I've created a road map for inviting people over to relax, nibble on something delicious, and join a great conversation (or maybe an ice-breaker game, page 37).

When I say, "Come over, let's have drinks and snacks on the patio!" it's one of the most intimate and low-pressure invites I can extend.

The moments we spend sitting around with friends, sipping Zesty Skinny Margaritas (page 162) and enjoying Green Chile and Spinach Artichoke Dip (page 142) or a luxurious cheese board (page 31) almost feel holy, don't they?

I KNOW IT SOUNDS CHEESY, BUT REVEALING OUR DEEPEST DESIRES, FREELY VENTING IN A SAFE SPACE, HEARING ABOUT SOMEONE'S LATEST HINGE DISASTER, CELEBRATING WINS, BONDING OVER LOSSES, AND LAUGHING WITH (AND AT) ONE ANOTHER ARE THE BEST TIMES.

Over the years, readers have told me their preferred way of entertaining is with easy-to-mix drinks and quick, snacky bites. And honestly, same here, GF.

While I love putting on a hyper-themed dinner party, I know it can seem a daunting undertaking to others. In contrast, throwing a happy hour at home is one of the most stress-free forms of hosting. In the following pages, you'll discover ideas for mixing and matching recipes for your own happy hour menu and learn how to mix cocktails (and lots of mocktails!) that come off as impressive but are super easy to make. Simply put, this book promises to take the edge off of having people over.

WELCOME TO HAPPY HOUR AT BAR ELIZABETH!

Bub and Grandma's
RESTAURANT & BAKERY

WHAT'S YOUR BEVERAGE STYLE?

STRONG

I LIKE SOMETHING STRONG AND LIQUOR-FORWARD

YOU LIKE A STRONG OUTFIT AND AN EVEN STRONGER DRINK

Dark & Sweet

- **DARK CHERRY WHISKEY SOUR**
- **BANANA CABANA COLD BREW**
- **HIBISCUS MEZCAL**

YOU LIKE ONE OR TWO DRINKS THAT HIT THE SPOT

Strong & Clean

- **VELVET SMOKE**
- **DIRTY MARTINI**
- **GIN MARTINI AND TONIC**
- **ZESTY SKINNY MARGARITA**

ZERO PROOF

I DON'T DRINK ALCOHOL BUT LOVE A FUN BEVERAGE

I LOVE IT WHEN A DRINK IS HYDRATING AND FLAVORFUL

Clean & Fresh

- **THE FAUXJITO**
- **NOAPEROL SPRITZ**
- **MEXICAN SUERO**

THIS IS A MOCKTAIL?! IT'S SO INTERESTING!

Fun & Inventive

- **KEY LIME PIE MATCHA**
- **THE GREEN KEY**
- **BLOODY MEREDITH**

FRUITY

I LIKE MY DRINKS SWEET AND FLAVORFUL

IF YOU LIKE SOUR CANDY AND TART DRINKS, HEAD THIS WAY

Citrus

- **THE VOGUE**
- **SQUIRT PALOMA**
- **PASSION FRUIT MARGARITA WITH TROPICAL FOAM**

IF YOU LIKE GIN AND SWEET DRINKS, HEAD THIS WAY

Floral

- **BACKYARD ORANGE GIN AND TONIC**
- **LYCHEE MARTINI**
- **PEACH WHITE LINEN**

BUBBLY

THE SPRITZ IS YOUR FIRST LOVE

YOU LOVE A CAFÉ IN ITALY SPRITZ MOMENT

Traditional Vibe

- **FRENCH 92**
- **LA DOLCE VITA MARGARITA**
- **FROZEN CHERRY LAMBRUSCO SPRITZ**

YOU LOVE WINE-BASED DRINKS

Wine Lover at Heart

- **BICICLETTA**
- **SUMMER SANGRIGIO**
- **NEW YORK SIDECAR**

LET'S PLAN YOUR HAPPY HOUR!
THE EASIEST WAY TO HOST

SET THE VIBE

Casual, always. Send out an eye-catching invite (I love a cute text graphic in Canva, but feel free to use your own preferred design tool) or a simple note that says to pop in between four and seven—you choose the time—for some tasty light bites and drinks. I like the idea of a recurring monthly happy hour—maybe the last Friday of every month?—which makes it feel like an at-home "special." If you're feeling creative, choose a fun theme, like tropical cabana night or drinks at the local dive bar.

Put on a great playlist. Dim the lights, or better yet, take everything outside and light a few candles for a cozy ambience. I like to set up a conversation space using comfy lounge furniture rather than a formal table. You can go as detailed or as loose with the decor as you wish.

If you want to spice things up, add a game or a fun conversation starter. The tray game (page 37) was my mom's go-to party game, and I carry on her hosting legacy with it to this day.

DRINKS

My rule of thumb is a tub of iced beer and/or wine and one batched drink. I'll also put out one or two types of soda or sparkling water, a full ice bucket, and a mix of drink garnishes. That pretty much covers all the bases.

For glassware, you can keep it really simple with a set of rocks glasses (for cocktails and NA drinks) and some wineglasses.

FOOD

I like to go with light, easy-to-graze-on dishes that are full of color and flavor. This book is filled with many of my favorites, including two of my most popular go-to recipes, Fancy Pigs in a Blanket (page 24) and Whipped Ricotta and Peach Crostini (page 58). Their components can be made a couple hours ahead of time and refrigerated, then assembled just before serving, making prep and setup a breeze.

Snacks! To bulk up the spread, I also put out a couple bowls of no-prep salty snacks, such as kettle chips, olives, and mixed nuts, and a wedge of cheese that I'm loving at the moment.

MENU

If you need a little more inspo, I've put together sample menus for Apericena (page 41), Drinks at the Hotel Bar (page 65), Holiday Hideaway (page 171), and Half Off at the Dive Bar (page 227) that simplify planning.

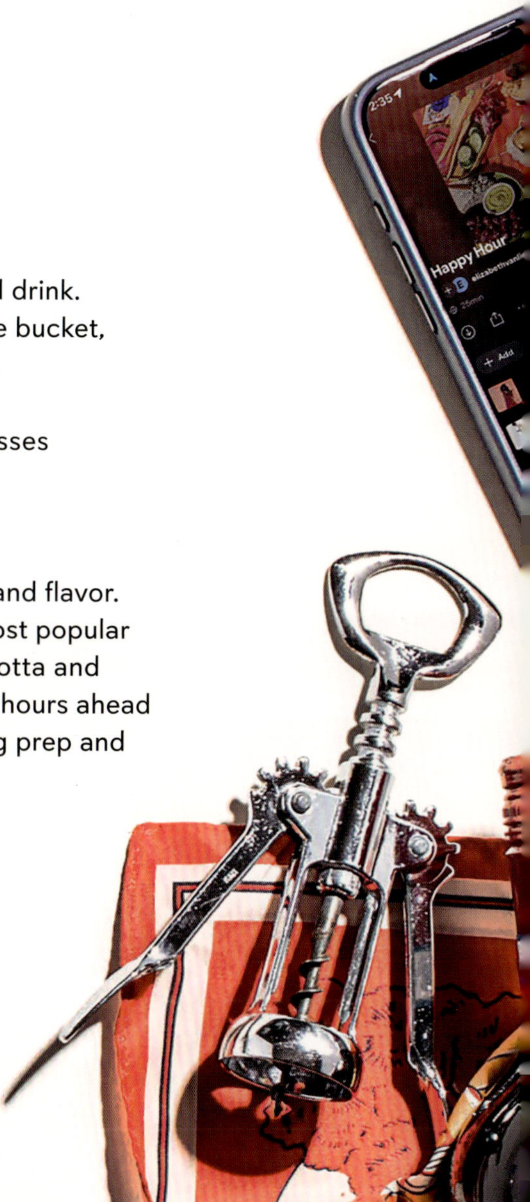

Premium
BEER
Ask For
INTO YOUR LIFE
Vos
Heineken
LIGHT
Old Milwaukee
BEER
Tastes as Great as its Name
STELLA ARTOIS
'n pils met karakter
speciaal voor u in Nederland gebrouwen

It's on the House

WHIPPED FETA DIP WITH SPICY CITRUS OLIVES

FOR THE FETA DIP

One 8-ounce block feta cheese, well drained and crumbled

¾ cup whole-milk plain Greek yogurt

2 tablespoons extra-virgin olive oil, plus more if needed

Grated zest of ½ lemon

2 teaspoons fresh lemon juice

Kosher salt

FOR THE OLIVES

½ cup pitted Castelvetrano olives, drained

2 tablespoons extra-virgin olive oil

2 garlic cloves, minced

1 tablespoon minced fresh rosemary leaves

Grated zest of ½ lemon

Grated zest of ½ orange

½ teaspoon red pepper flakes

Crackers, crusty bread slices, and raw vegetables (such as cucumber slices, celery sticks, radishes, and red bell pepper strips), for serving

SERVES 6

This is one of those appetizers that as soon as you put it on the table, guests dig in, finishing it off within minutes. The fluffy feta dip has a bit of a kick that makes it downright addicting, and it's topped with citrus-marinated olives for extra brightness and texture. I love having a dip like this prepped and ready to go in the refrigerator. That way, I know that as soon as my guests arrive, I've got something wonderful to serve them.

TO MAKE THE FETA DIP, in a food processor, combine the feta, yogurt, olive oil, and lemon zest and juice and process for 20 to 30 seconds, or until the mixture is smooth and fluffy. Add more olive oil, 1 teaspoon at a time, if needed to achieve the correct consistency. Taste and add salt if needed (the feta may provide enough saltiness).

Transfer the dip to a shallow bowl and, using a rubber spatula or wooden spoon, create a circular pattern. Cover and refrigerate until serving. (The dip can be made up to 8 hours in advance.)

TO MAKE THE OLIVES, in a small bowl, combine the olives, olive oil, garlic, rosemary, lemon zest, orange zest, and pepper flakes and stir and toss until well mixed. Let sit for about 15 minutes for the flavors to blend.

Top the dip with the olives, arranging them in a swirl or pile, and serve with the crackers, chunks of bread, and/or fresh vegetables.

ELIZABETH'S TIP

This dip pairs well with a round of Dirty Martinis (page 28). Set aside a few of the olives for spearing on cocktail picks for a quick and tasty drink garnish.

DARK CHERRY WHISKEY SOUR

2 Luxardo or Tillen Farms Merry maraschino cherries

2 ounces bourbon

1 ounce fresh lemon juice

½ ounce fresh orange juice

1 ounce syrup from Luxardo or Tillen Farms Merry cherries

Orange slice or wheel and/or maraschino cherries, for garnish

SERVES 1

One of my goals for this book is to teach you how to make a damn good cocktail with each of the five main spirits. I always make this fruity variation on a classic whiskey sour for my whiskey-loving guests. But if I've learned anything over the years, it is that "most" guys will order a whiskey drink to feel masculine but end up drinking the fruit-forward cocktail I've made for their wives. So gentlemen, this flavorful, slightly sweet whiskey sour is the best of both worlds.

Put the maraschino cherries into a cocktail shaker and muddle until they are smashed and have released their juices. Add the bourbon, lemon juice, orange juice, cherry juice, and 2 scoops of ice. Cover the shaker and shake hard for 10 to 15 seconds, or until the outside of the shaker is frosty cold to the touch.

Strain into a rocks glass over ice. Garnish with the orange slice and/or maraschino cherries.

FANCY PIGS IN A BLANKET

FOR THE HONEY-MUSTARD GLAZE

1 tablespoon unsalted butter

2 tablespoons honey

1 tablespoon brown sugar

1 tablespoon Dijon mustard

1 teaspoon Worcestershire sauce

½ teaspoon garlic powder

1 tablespoon chopped fresh rosemary leaves

One 8-ounce tube crescent rolls

24 fully cooked cocktail wieners

Kosher salt

Dijon mustard and ketchup, for serving

MAKES 24 PIECES

There is an art to creating food that tastes both elevated and nostalgic in the same bite. These old-school appetizers are a good example of doing just that. It never ceases to amaze me how people's eyes light up when a plate of these pigs in a blanket is set on the table. One bite and I know I've tapped into their child selves. Prep them ahead of time (see Elizabeth's Tip) and bake them off right before your guests arrive.

TO MAKE THE GLAZE, in a small saucepan, mix together the butter, honey, brown sugar, mustard, Worcestershire sauce, garlic powder, and rosemary until smooth. Place over medium heat and cook, stirring occasionally, for 3 to 4 minutes, or until the sugar has dissolved and the glaze is smooth and slightly thickened. Remove from the heat and set aside.

Open the tube of crescent rolls and unroll the dough on a cutting board. Cut along the perforated lines in the dough to create 8 triangles. Then, starting at the wide end of each triangle, cut the triangle lengthwise into 3 equal triangles. You should have 24 triangles.

Place a wiener on the wide end of a dough triangle and roll up the wiener in the dough. Repeat with the remaining wieners and dough triangles.

TO COOK IN AN AIR FRYER, preheat the air fryer to 330°F. You will need to cook them in two or three batches, depending on the size of your air fryer. Place the "pigs" in a single layer in the air fryer basket, spacing them about 1 inch apart, and cook for 3 to 4 minutes. Brush the tops with the glaze, sprinkle lightly with salt, and continue to cook for 2 to 3 minutes, or until the tops are golden brown.

TO COOK IN THE OVEN, preheat the oven to 375°F. Line two 9-by-13-inch sheet pans with parchment paper. Arrange half of the pigs in a blanket on each prepared sheet pan, arranging them in four evenly spaced rows. Bake for 5 to 6 minutes, or until they begin to color. Remove the pans from the oven, brush the tops with the glaze, and sprinkle lightly with salt. Return the pans to the oven and bake for 5 to 6 minutes, or until the tops are golden brown.

Transfer the pigs in a blanket to a platter and serve hot. Accompany with the mustard and ketchup for dipping.

ELIZABETH'S TIP

The day before the party, wrap the wieners in the dough, arrange them on a sheet pan lined with parchment paper, cover tightly with plastic wrap, and refrigerate, then let the pan sit out on the counter while you preheat the air fryer or the oven.

NEGRONI
BOMBAY
Distilled
LONDON
DRY GIN
Vapour
INFUSED
LEMON DROP
VODKA
FAMILY MADE
AT THE
NOLET DISTILLERY
MARTINI
DIRTY MART
EXTRA DRY
VERMOUTH

BATCHED CLASSICS

These big batch cocktails provide a taste for everyone's palate. The self-serve bar station is great for easy entertaining. Use your old liquor bottles or glass carafes as containers. Add glassware, a bowl of fresh citrus fruits, a full ice bucket, and a couple of jiggers for measuring and let your guests do the rest. The bottles will keep in your freezer door, which means you'll always have a craft cocktail at your fingertips.

DIRTY MARTINIS

16 ounces gin

6 ounces olive brine

2 ounces vermouth

2 tablespoons water

Green cocktail olives, for garnish

A dirty gin martini is a welcome addition to nearly any drinks list. Serve these perfectly briny drinks with the spicy olives on page 20.

In an empty gin bottle or other similar-size glass container with a tight cap, combine the gin, olive brine, vermouth, and water. Cap tightly, turn it upside down a few times to mix the ingredients, and place in the freezer for an hour or more to chill well.

When ready to serve, pour into chilled martini glasses. Garnish each glass with a cocktail pick of olives.

LEMON DROPS

8 ounces vodka

8 ounces fresh lemon juice

4 ounces simple syrup

4 ounces Cointreau or other orange liqueur

Lemon twists, for garnish

If I've learned anything in my home bartending days, it's that the gurls are always down for a tart-and-sweet lemon drop.

In an empty vodka bottle or other similar-size glass container with a tight cap, combine the vodka, lemon juice, simple syrup, and Cointreau. Cap tightly, turn it upside down a few times to mix the ingredients, then place in the freezer for an hour or more to chill well.

When ready to serve, for each lemon drop, pour about 4 ounces into a cocktail shaker. Add 2 scoops of ice, cover the shaker, and shake hard for 10 to 15 seconds, or until the outside of the shaker is frosty to the touch. Strain into a chilled martini or coupe glass and garnish with a lemon twist.

NEGRONIS

8 ounces gin

8 ounces Campari

8 ounces sweet red vermouth

Orange peel, for garnish

EACH BATCH SERVES 8

A negroni makes a great liquor-forward cocktail for guests who love something bitter yet balanced with both sweet and herbal notes.

In an empty gin bottle or other similar-size glass container with a tight cap, combine the gin, Campari, and vermouth. Cap tightly, turn it upside down a few times to mix the ingredients, then place in the freezer for an hour or more to chill well.

When ready to serve, for each negroni, fill a mixing glass about two-thirds full with ice. Pour about 3 ounces of the negroni mix into the glass, then, using a barspoon, stir around the edge of the glass about twenty times, or until well chilled. Strain into a rocks glass over a large ice cube and garnish with an orange peel.

HOUSE CHEESE BOARD

2 ounces Kingston Creamery blue cheese

2 ounces Somerdale Cooper's Hill British double Gloucester with onion and chives

3½ ounces Cowgirl Creamery Mt Tam or other triple cream Brie

4 ounce Trader Joe's Blueberry Vanilla Chèvre

Tarragon Dijon mustard

Honey

Fig jam

2 ounces sliced prosciutto or salami

Marcona almonds

Soft dried apricots (I like Mariani brand)

Honeycrisp apple slices

Champagne grapes

About 8 ounces assorted favorite crackers (I like Carr's Entertainment Crackers Collection)

Rosemary sprigs, for garnish

SERVES 4 TO 6

I get asked quite a bit about how to put together the perfect charcuterie board, and my best tip is to try lots of cheeses and keep a running list of the ones you enjoyed on your refrigerator. That way, you always know what to go back to. This is my personal list of cheeses and snacks that are longstanding house favorites and great for any season.

Grab a medium cheese board or serving tray. Use the cheese pieces as the anchors, placing them on four different sections of the board or tray.

Put the mustard, honey, and jam into separate small serving bowls and space them evenly around the board or tray. Fill in the remaining areas with the prosciutto, almonds, apricots, apple slices, grapes, and crackers. Garnish the board or tray with rosemary sprigs and set a few cheese knives and spreaders alongside.

FROZEN MARGARITAS 3 WAYS

If your favorite place to host is your backyard (mine too!), a fruit-flavored frozen margarita is the perfect menu staple. Here are three great variations to get you started. Then feel free to experiment with other fruits, from raspberries and blackberries to watermelon and mango. This recipe formula can be used for other frozen cocktails too. Just trade out the tequila for a liquor you prefer (vodka works great and is neutral in flavor).

EACH BATCH SERVES 4

Tajín and lime wedge, for rimming the glasses

STRAWBERRY MARGARITA

One 16-ounce bag frozen strawberries

4 ounces fresh lime juice

8 ounces silver (blanco) tequila

4 ounces Cointreau

2 ounces agave nectar (optional)

2 cups ice

Fresh strawberries, for garnish

PINEAPPLE MARGARITA

One 16-ounce bag frozen pineapple chunks

4 ounces fresh lime juice

4 ounces pineapple juice

8 ounces silver (blanco) tequila

4 ounces Cointreau

2 ounces agave nectar (optional)

2 cups ice

Fresh pineapple wedges, for garnish

PEACH MARGARITA

One 16-ounce bag frozen sliced peaches

4 ounces fresh lime juice

8 ounces silver (blanco) tequila

4 ounces Cointreau

2 ounces agave nectar (optional)

2 cups ice

Fresh peach slices, for garnish

Pour a thin layer of Tajín onto a flat saucer. Dampen the outside rim of a cocktail glass with the lime wedge, then holding the glass at an angle almost parallel to the saucer, roll the dampened edge in the Tajín to coat lightly. Set the glass aside. Repeat with 3 more cocktail glasses for each batch.

Each margarita batch—strawberry, pineapple, and peach—is made the same way. In a blender, combine all the ingredients, including the agave nectar (if using), and blend on high speed until smooth. Taste and adjust the sweetness with agave nectar if needed.

Pour into the Tajín-rimmed glasses and garnish with the fresh fruit.

LEMON COOKIE TART

FOR THE CRUST

About 28 Lorna Doone shortbread cookies (from seven 4-cookie packs or five 6-cookie packs)

2 tablespoons sugar

4 tablespoons unsalted butter, melted

½ teaspoon kosher salt

FOR THE FILLING

4 egg yolks

One 14-ounce can sweetened condensed milk

½ cup fresh lemon juice, strained (about 3 lemons)

FOR THE WHIPPED CREAM

1 cup heavy cream

1 tablespoon sugar

Pinch of kosher salt

Grated lemon zest, for garnish

SERVES 8

ELIZABETH'S TIP

I love giving happy hours a silly theme. Invite your friends over to the "Lemon Drop Lounge" for Lemon Drops (page 28) and this unforgettable lemon tart.

The recipe for Key Lime pie in my first book, *Everyday Entertaining*, was a big fan and house favorite. This new lemon tart is a play on that success but a little more nostalgic. The filling is a velvety lemon cream, and the crust is made with crushed Lorna Doone cookies. The striking green-and-yellow Lorna Doone cookie box is ingrained in my childhood memory. My grandma and my mom always had packs of the buttery shortbread cookies in their pantries.

Preheat the oven to 350°F.

TO MAKE THE CRUST, put the cookies into a food processor and pulse until reduced to fine crumbs. Alternatively, put the cookies into a large resealable bag, secure the bag closed, and crush with a wine bottle or rolling pin to fine crumbs. You should have 1½ cups cookie crumbs.

In a medium bowl, stir together the cookie crumbs, sugar, butter, and salt until the crumbs are evenly moistened.

Transfer the crumb mixture to a 10-inch round tart pan. Using your fingers, press the crumb mixture evenly across the bottom and up the sides of the pan.

Place the tart pan on a sheet pan and bake the crust for 12 to 15 minutes, or until lightly browned and fragrant. Let cool completely on the sheet pan on a wire rack while you prepare the filing.

TO MAKE THE FILLING, in a stand mixer fitted with the paddle attachment, or in a medium bowl with a handheld mixer, beat the egg yolks on high speed until pale yellow. Add the condensed milk and lemon juice and beat on medium speed until well blended.

Pour the filling into the cooled tart crust. Bake for 15 to 17 minutes, or until the edges of the filling are set and the center jiggles just slightly when the pan is shaken. Let cool in the pan on a wire rack for 30 minutes, then cover and refrigerate for 4 to 6 hours, or until fully cooled and firm.

TO MAKE THE WHIPPED CREAM, in the stand mixer fitted with the whisk attachment, or in a medium bowl with a handheld mixer, beat together the cream, sugar, and salt on medium-high speed until medium peaks form. Cover and refrigerate until serving.

To serve, cut the tart into slices and accompany each slice with a dollop of whipped cream garnished with lemon zest.

dvance Single
York
London Kings Cross
CUSTOMER
02-MAY-24
KIKKOMAN
TRADITIONALLY BREWED
Soy Sauce
BREWED IN U.S.A.
le mini macaron
nail lacquer
GINNY
SUPER GLUE
SUPER GOMA
REPLICA
Maison Margiela
PARIS
Milwaukee
6FT/2m
HEINZ
YELLOW MUSTARD

The Tray Game

HOW TO PLAY

This is an extremely easy and fun last-minute game to put together. My mom would always play it with us on holidays and at birthday parties, and it's a good way to get everyone active and a little competitive. Plus, you pretty much need zero supplies! You can tailor the tray items to any theme or number of people.

1. Grab a tray or a serving platter and fill it with 30 to 40 small-to-medium-size items. The more abstract the items the better!

2. Give everyone 30 to 60 seconds to get a good look at the tray (no touching!) and then remove the tray from the room.

3. Hand each player a small notepad and a pen and tell them to write down as many items as they can remember in 30 seconds. Whoever has the most correct items on their list gets either a fun prize or just bragging rights and a cocktail of their choice.

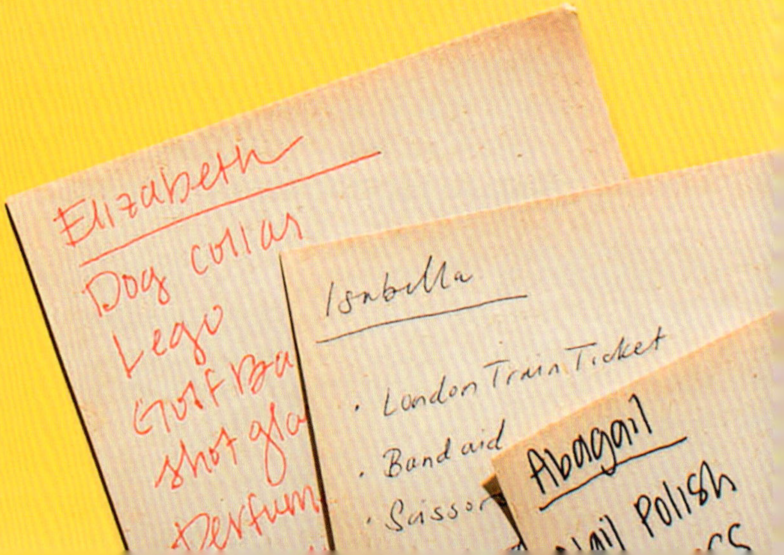

BACKYARD ORANGE GIN AND TONIC

1½ ounces gin

½ ounce St-Germain elderflower liqueur

1 ounce fresh orange juice

2 dashes orange bitters

2 to 3 ounces tonic water, preferably Fever-Tree

Orange blossom and orange slice, for garnish

SERVES 1

As a California-born and -raised girl, I can measure the seasons based on whatever fruit is falling off the trees in the backyard. These orange gin and tonics were born from an abundance of oranges from our tree. We had an impromptu happy hour, and although that backyard harvest was pretty much all I had to work with, I soon realized it pointed toward a great citrusy riff on the gin and tonic. Made with freshly squeezed orange juice and a splash of elderflower liqueur, this is truly sunshine in a glass.

In a highball glass, combine the gin, elderflower liqueur, orange juice, and orange bitters and stir gently. Fill the glass with ice. Top with the tonic water and stir once more. Garnish with the orange blossom and orange slice.

Apericena

LA DOLCE VITA MARGARITA

Kosher salt, grated orange zest, and orange wedge, for rimming the glass

1 ounce Aperol

2 ounces silver (blanco) tequila

1 ounce fresh lemon juice

1 ounce fresh blood orange juice

½ to 1 ounce agave nectar

SERVES 1

On a hot summer night, some drinks make you want to put on a short sundress and clip up your hair into a messy bun, and this margarita is one of them. She's sexy, juicy, and slightly bitter. Triple sec has been traded out for Aperol, creating not only a stunning color but also a bold Italian flavor. Give this one a try with a round of girlfriends and live in the moment for the night.

Mix a thin layer of salt and orange zest on a flat saucer. Rub the outside rim of a rocks glass with the orange wedge, then holding the glass at an angle almost parallel to the plate, roll the dampened edge in the salt mixture to coat lightly. Set the glass aside.

In a cocktail shaker, combine the Aperol, tequila, lemon juice, blood orange juice, and agave nectar (use the larger amount for a sweeter sip). Add 2 scoops ice, cover the shaker, and shake hard for 10 to 15 seconds, or until the outside of the shaker feels frosty cold to the touch.

Fill the salt-rimmed glass with ice and strain the cocktail into the glass. Garnish with the orange wedge.

CHICKEN MILANESE BITES WITH GARLIC AIOLI

FOR THE GARLIC AIOLI

½ cup mayonnaise

1 teaspoon Dijon mustard

½ teaspoon anchovy paste

1 teaspoon Worcestershire sauce

2 garlic cloves, grated

Grated zest of ½ lemon, plus 1 tablespoon lemon juice

¼ cup grated Parmigiano-Reggiano cheese

FOR THE ARUGULA SALAD

2 cups arugula

1 cup cherry tomatoes, halved

1 tablespoon extra-virgin olive oil

Juice of ½ lemon

Kosher salt and ground black pepper

FOR THE CHICKEN BITES

1 pound boneless, skinless chicken breasts, cut into 1-inch cubes

Kosher salt and ground black pepper

5 tablespoons all-purpose flour

3 eggs

1 cup panko bread crumbs

¼ cup grated Parmigiano-Reggiano cheese, plus more for serving

½ teaspoon garlic powder

1½ teaspoons Italian seasoning

½ cup olive oil

2 lemons

SERVES 4 TO 6

If you're a chicken nugget kind of girl, it is imperative that you try these crispy, golden Milanese-inspired bites. They are served with a zesty arugula salad and a rich, garlicky dipping sauce that is practically drinkable.

TO MAKE THE DIPPING SAUCE, in a small bowl, whisk together the mayonnaise, mustard, anchovy paste, Worcestershire sauce, grated garlic, lemon zest and juice, and cheese until smooth. Cover and set aside. (The sauce can be made up to 2 hours in advance, covered, and refrigerated.)

TO MAKE THE ARUGULA SALAD, in a medium bowl, combine the arugula and tomatoes and toss to mix. Drizzle with the olive oil and lemon juice, then top with a sprinkle of salt and a few grinds of pepper and toss to mix. Cover and refrigerate until serving.

TO MAKE THE CHICKEN BITES, sprinkle the chicken cubes on all sides with salt and pepper, dropping them into a medium bowl as you work. Then sprinkle the seasoned chicken cubes with the flour and toss to coat evenly. Line up two small shallow bowls next to the bowl of chicken cubes. In the first bowl, whisk the eggs. In the second bowl, stir together the panko, cheese, garlic powder, and Italian seasoning. Have ready a large plate for the chicken bites.

One at a time, dip each floured chicken cube into the egg, letting the excess drip off (use a fork to help keep your hands clean), and then into the panko mixture, coating evenly and pressing with your fingertips so the crumbs adhere. As each piece is ready, place it on the plate.

Line a large plate with paper towels and set it near the stovetop. Halve a lemon and set it nearby. Heat the olive oil in heavy medium skillet over medium heat until a few bread crumbs dropped into it sizzle on contact. Working in batches, add the chicken cubes in a single layer, not touching, and cook for about 2 minutes on each side, or until golden brown all over and an instant-read thermometer inserted into a cube registers 165°F. Transfer to the towel-lined plate and top with a sprinkle of salt and a squeeze or two of lemon juice.

Cut the remaining lemon into wedges. Serve the chicken bites right away with the salad, garlic aioli, and lemon wedges. Sprinkle the salad with Parmigiano-Reggiano.

Menu

Apericena lives somewhere between happy hour and dinner. Light bites and dishes that can be eaten with your hands or buffet style. To create your own Apericena, select a medley of 1 to 2 cocktails and 2 to 3 bites and snacks to serve.

Buon Appetito!

SPICY RIGATONI

1 tablespoon extra-virgin olive oil

2 garlic cloves, thinly sliced

1 shallot, diced

2 tablespoons tomato paste

1 teaspoon red pepper flakes, plus more for topping

2 cups sweet cherry tomatoes

12 ounces rigatoni pasta

1 cup heavy cream

1½ teaspoons kosher salt

Grated Parmigiano-Reggiano cheese, for finishing

SERVES 4 AS A MAIN COURSE OR 6 AS A LIGHT BITE

An apericena menu wouldn't be complete without an incredibly easy and delectable pasta recipe. This dish of al dente rigatoni cloaked in a silky, spicy tomato sauce and topped with plenty of Parmigiano-Reggiano fills that menu slot perfectly. I'm going to say something *very* bold: This spicy pasta and a La Dolce Vita Margarita (page 43) is one of my favorite pairings in this book.

Fill a large pot three-fourths full with generously salted water and bring to a boil over high heat.

While the water is heating, set a large, heavy skillet over medium heat. Add the olive oil and heat for 1 to 2 minutes, or until the oil is shimmering. Add the garlic and shallot and cook, stirring often, for about 2 minutes, or until softened. Turn down the heat to medium-low, stir in the tomato paste and pepper flakes, and cook, stirring, for 1 minute.

Add the cherry tomatoes and cook, stirring occasionally, for 3 to 4 minutes, or until the tomatoes have softened. Press down on the tomatoes with a wooden spoon to release their juices, then continue to cook, stirring occasionally, for 5 to 6 minutes longer, or until the sauce has thickened slightly.

While the sauce is cooking, add the rigatoni to the boiling water, stir well, and cook for 12 to 14 minutes, or according to package directions for al dente. Drain the pasta into a colander.

Add the cream and salt to the skillet and stir well. Transfer the sauce to a blender, let cool briefly, and then blend until smooth and creamy. Return the sauce to the skillet over low heat. (Alternatively, blend the sauce directly in the pan with an immersion blender.)

Add the hot cooked pasta to the skillet and stir and toss until evenly coated with the sauce. Transfer to a serving platter, top with a shower of cheese and a dusting of pepper flakes, and serve.

BICICLETTA

2 ounces Campari

3 ounces white wine, such as Pinot Grigio or Sauvignon Blanc

2 ounces Italian lemon soda or soda water

Orange wheel or orange peel, for garnish

SERVES 1

Legend has it that the bicicletta is named after the sight of older Italian gentlemen heading home—their bicycles swerving and wobbling along the roadway—after a few too many drinks at the local bar (aka café). A tipsy bike ride home with your friends in the Italian countryside? Count me in. The Italians really just do it better. A drink cousin to the Aperol spritz, a bicicletta swaps Aperol for Campari and prosecco for white wine. Easy to make, and even easier to drink.

In a wineglass or cocktail glass, combine the Campari and wine. Add ice cubes to fill the glass, then top with the soda and stir gently to mix. Garnish with the orange wheel.

MB

SUMMER SANGRIGIO

FOR THE BASIL SIMPLE SYRUP

½ cup sugar

½ cup water

1 cup fresh basil leaves

FOR THE SANGRIA

One 750-ml bottle Pinot Grigio or other dry white wine

4 ounces peach liqueur

4 ounces vodka

2 ounces fresh lemon juice

2 ounces basil simple syrup

1 peach, halved, pitted, and sliced

1 cup strawberries, hulled and sliced

1¾ cups raspberries

SERVES 4 TO 6

Isn't Summer Sangrigio the perfect name for this light, refreshing sangria? I promise the seasonal flavors will win you over. The base of this crisp white wine punch is Pinot Grigio (see where I went there?), which gets a zesty kick from a big splash of vodka, fruity notes from peach slices and berries, and a touch of herbal sweetness from a basil-infused simple syrup.

TO MAKE THE BASIL SIMPLE SYRUP, in a small saucepan over medium-low heat, combine the sugar, water, and basil and bring to a simmer, stirring until the sugar has completely dissolved. Remove from the heat and let steep for 20 to 30 minutes, or until fragrant and flavorful. Drain through a fine-mesh strainer into a small glass jar. Discard the spent basil and set the syrup aside to cool completely. You should have about ¾ cup. It will keep tightly capped in the refrigerator for up to 1 month.

TO MAKE THE SANGRIA, in a 2-quart pitcher, combine the wine, peach liqueur, vodka, lemon juice, and simple syrup and stir to mix. Add the peach slices, strawberries, and raspberries, then stir again, cover, and refrigerate for at least 8 hours or preferably overnight.

Serve the sangria over ice in large wineglasses or goblets. Provide spoons for scooping up the fruits.

ELIZABETH'S TIP

Feel free to use an inexpensive ($10 or less) bottle of wine. The fresh fruit will instantly bring out fresh notes and make each sip taste robust.

FROZEN CHERRY LAMBRUSCO SPRITZ

12 ounces Lambrusco wine, chilled

12 ounces citrus vodka or regular vodka, chilled

3 ounces fresh orange juice

One 16-ounce bag frozen cherries

1 cup lemon sorbet

2 cups ice cubes

Castelvetrano olives and/or orange slices, for garnish

SERVES 4 TO 6

If there was a red-wine prosecco, Lambrusco would be its first cousin. Bubbly, fruity, and slightly sweet, it makes a great base for this delightful frozen spritz, which is like frosé and red wine sangria joined forces to make the best wine slush you will ever drink. With notes of fresh citrus, sweet cherries, and a strong finish, this is one of my favorite sips for the hottest of summer days.

In a blender, combine the wine, vodka, orange juice, cherries, sorbet, and ice and pulse until the ice breaks up a bit, then blend until smooth.

Divide among four to six cocktail glasses. Garnish each spritz with an olive, an orange slice, or both.

ELIZABETH'S TIP

For the smoothest frozen texture, put all the ingredients in the blender jar and chill the jar in the freezer for 30 to 60 minutes. Then blend the batch when you're ready to serve.

LAPO'S
750 ML
SICILIANA
MONATA
di Sicilia
Lemon Soda

NOPEROL SPRITZ

3 ounces nonalcoholic aperitif, preferably Lapo's (see Elizabeth's Tip)

3 ounces nonalcoholic prosecco or other sparkling wine

2 ounces sparkling lemonade

Orange slice, for garnish

SERVES 1

A great addition to your apericena drink lineup, the Noperol Spritz is my lower-calorie, no-alcohol alternative to the Aperol spritz. It's just as easy to make as its almost namesake, and its flavor profile is surprisingly and pleasantly similar to the fan favorite.

Fill a large wineglass with ice. Pour in the aperitif, prosecco, and lemonade and stir gently. Garnish with the orange slice.

APEROL SPRITZ

3 ounces prosecco

1 to 2 ounces Aperol

1 to 2 ounces club soda

Orange slice, for garnish

SERVES 1

I love giving my guests the option of cocktail or zero proof. This is how I make a classic Aperol spritz.

Fill a large wineglass with ice. Pour in the prosecco and Aperol and stir gently. Top with the club soda and again stir gently. Garnish with the orange slice.

ELIZABETH'S TIP

Nonalcoholic aperitifs are becoming easier to find. For this mocktail, I like the Italian-made Lapo's aperitivo, a heady mix of citrus-forward and earthy botanicals that I found at a local Total Wine & More. Target also carries a good selection of nonalcoholic aperitifs.

WHIPPED RICOTTA AND PEACH CROSTINI

FOR THE WHIPPED RICOTTA
2 cups whole-milk ricotta cheese (one 15-ounce container)

2 tablespoons extra-virgin olive oil

4 teaspoons honey

Grated zest of 1 lemon

½ teaspoon kosher salt

FOR THE TOASTS
12 slices Italian semolina bread or 24 baguette slices, each about ½ inch thick

Extra-virgin olive oil, for drizzling

Flaky sea salt

6 thin prosciutto slices

1 peach, halved, pitted, and diced

Honey, for drizzling

Fresh basil leaves, chopped or torn, for topping

Flaky sea salt, for topping

MAKES 12 LARGE OR 24 SMALL CROSTINI

I have found that any kind of whipped cheese is an instant house favorite, making these crostini a must on any apericena menu. Each bite is a bit sweet from the juicy peaches and a little salty from the crispy prosciutto. I like to use a traditional rustic Italian semolina loaf for the toasts, but you can swap out the semolina bread for baguette slices.

TO MAKE THE WHIPPED RICOTTA, in a food processor, combine the ricotta, olive oil, honey, lemon zest, and kosher salt and process until smooth and fluffy. Transfer to piping bag fitted with a ½-inch round tip or to a ziplock plastic bag, secure the bag closed, and refrigerate until the toasts are ready.

TO MAKE THE TOASTS, preheat the oven to 400°F. Line a large sheet pan with parchment paper.

Arrange the bread slices in a single layer on the prepared sheet pan. Drizzle the tops lightly with olive oil and sprinkle with flaky salt.

Bake for 3 to 4 minutes, or until the tops are golden, and then flip each toast. Continue baking for about 3 minutes longer, or until golden brown on the second side. Remove from the oven and transfer the toasts to a serving platter to finish cooling. Leave the oven on.

Lay the prosciutto slices flat on the same parchment-lined pan. Bake for 12 to 14 minutes, or until crispy. Remove from the oven and let cool completely on the pan on a wire rack. Once cooled, crumble the prosciutto into small pieces.

Just before serving, assemble the crostini. If using a resealable bag for piping the ricotta, snip off a lower corner. Pipe an even swirl of the ricotta onto each toast, dividing it evenly. Top each swirl with some peach pieces, a drizzle of honey, a scattering of basil, a bit of crumbled prosciutto, and a sprinkle of flaky salt. If you have used semolina bread slices, cut each toast in half if you like. Serve right away.

ELIZABETH'S TIP

If you're short on time, you can use the whipped ricotta as a dip. Top it with the peach pieces, crumbled prosciutto, a drizzle of honey, a little basil, and a sprinkle of flaky salt and serve with the toasts for dipping.

LIMONJELLO SHOTS

6 large lemons

1 cup water

4 teaspoons (2 envelopes) unflavored gelatin powder

1 cup sugar

2 ounces limoncello

8 ounces vodka

MAKES 24 JELL-O SHOTS

I promise you that Jell-O shots don't have to be tacky. Here, fresh lemons are halved and then hollowed out to hold these tart-sweet Jell-O bites (goodbye, plastic condiment cups). I love whipping out a tray of these boozy treats to get any evening started. If your friends are anything like mine, they'll not only love how dainty and picture-perfect they look but also how deliciously lemony and smooth they are going down.

Cut the lemons in half lengthwise. Using a spoon with a pointed bowl, scoop out the insides from each lemon half into a small bowl. Arrange the lemon halves, hollow sides up, in a baking dish in which they fit snugly or tuck each one into the well of a muffin pan. This will ensure easy transfer in and out of refrigerator later.

Express the lemon juice from the lemon insides, then strain the juice through a fine-mesh strainer into a measuring cup. You should have ¾ cup.

Measure the 1 cup water in a measuring cup and sprinkle the gelatin lightly and evenly on top of the water. Allow the gelatin to "bloom" (the granules will visibly swell) for 5 to 10 minutes. This "blooming" step ensures your shots will have a silky Jell-O texture.

Pour the water-gelatin mixture into a small saucepan and place over medium-low heat. Once the mixture is warm, slowly whisk in the sugar and continue to whisk over medium-low heat just until the sugar is fully dissolved. Set aside for 5 to 10 minutes to cool slightly.

Add the reserved ¾ cup lemon juice, the limoncello, and the vodka to a medium glass measuring pitcher with a spout and stir to mix. Slowly pour the gelatin-sugar mixture into the lemon juice mixture while stirring constantly to mix well.

Pour the lemon-gelatin mixture into the lemon halves, dividing it evenly. Cover and refrigerate for at least 4 to 6 hours or up to overnight to allow the shots to set fully.

Once the shots are set, cut each lemon half in half to create a pair of lemon "wedges," then arrange on a platter or board and serve.

Drinks at the Hotel Bar

LYCHEE MARTINI

2 ounces vodka

1 ounce syrup from a can of lychees

½ ounce fresh lime juice

½ ounce St-Germain elderflower liqueur

Fresh lychee, peeled, and/or edible flowers, such as orchid or hibiscus, for garnish

SERVES 1

Light, floral, and delicately sweet, this drink feels like the quiet luxury of a grand hotel but is actually super easy to make at home. Pick up a can of lychees in sweet syrup and some limes and be sure you have vodka and elderflower liqueur in your liquor cabinet. I like to garnish this delicate vodka martini with an orchid flower for an extra-chic touch, but you can also use other edible flowers, lime peel, or fresh mint.

In a cocktail shaker, combine the vodka, lychee syrup, lime juice, and elderflower liqueur. Add 2 scoops of ice, cover the shaker, and shake hard for 10 to 15 seconds, or until the outside of the shaker is frosty cold to the touch.

Strain into a chilled martini glass. Garnish with the lychee and flowers.

ELIZABETH'S TIP

Not all canned lychees are the same. Make sure you grab a can labeled "lychees in syrup" so the drink turns out sweet enough. If you pick up lychees in water or juice, your martini will be watery and lack flavor.

Come Stay Awhile

HOTEL BAR SNACK MIX

½ cup (1 stick) unsalted butter, melted and cooled

One 1-ounce packet dry ranch dressing mix

2 tablespoons light brown sugar

1½ tablespoons Worcestershire sauce

½ teaspoon red pepper flakes

2 cups Corn Chex or Wheat Chex cereal

1½ cups oyster crackers

1 cup Goldfish crackers

1 cup Cheez-It crackers

1 cup mini pretzels

1 cup Marcona almonds

SERVES 6 TO 8

When you were a kid (or adult, ha!), did you go crazy for the warm chocolate chip cookies in every DoubleTree by Hilton hotel lobby like I did? If I had a hotel, this would be my signature lobby snack mix. It's a fun blend of such youthful favorites as Cheez-It and Goldfish crackers combined with Marcona almonds and a buttery ranch seasoning. This addictive combo is especially great for noshing on alongside a stiff cocktail.

Preheat the oven to 300°F.

In a large bowl, combine the melted butter, ranch dressing mix, sugar, Worcestershire sauce, and pepper flakes and stir until the dressing mix and sugar dissolve and all the ingredients are well mixed.

Add the Corn Chex, oyster crackers, Goldfish crackers, Cheez-It crackers, pretzels, and almonds to the butter mixture and stir together until all the ingredients are evenly coated with the butter mixture.

Turn the mixture out onto a large sheet pan and spread it evenly on the pan. Most of the ingredients should not overlap one another. (If necessary, position two oven racks in the center of the oven, divide the snack mix between two smaller sheet pans, place a pan on each rack, and then switch the pans between the racks about midway through baking to ensure even baking.)

Bake, tossing the ingredients every 10 minutes, for about 30 minutes, or until aromatic and lightly toasted.

Transfer the snack mix to a bowl and serve warm or at room temperature. The snack mix will keep in an airtight container at room temperature for up to 1 week.

VELVET SMOKE

1 ounce reposado (aged) tequila

1 ounce mezcal

1 teaspoon agave nectar

2 dashes chocolate bitters

Orange peel and small dark-chocolate square, for garnish

SERVES 1

This sultry nightcap lives in that late-night hour when the hotel bar lights dim and the evening is slowing down. Its velvety cocoa notes from chocolate bitters and smoky mezcal are meant to mimic that little luxury of finding a chocolate on your pillow when you stumble into your hotel room. Sip this slowly like you would an old fashioned, or it will hit you straight in the heart.

Put a large ice cube into a rocks glass. Add the tequila, mezcal, agave nectar, and bitters and stir gently until well chilled.

Alternatively, in a mixing glass, combine the tequila, mezcal, agave nectar, and bitters. Fill the glass two-thirds full with ice, then, using a barspoon, stir around the edge of the glass twenty to thirty times, or until well chilled. Strain into a rocks glass over a large ice cube.

Garnish with the orange peel. Serve the chocolate square in a small bowl on the side.

PRALINE

Menu

Low candles, crisp marble countertops, a silver bowl of French fries (with extra ketchup for me), and bottomless martinis are exactly how I like my hotel bar order. Create this late-night feeling anywhere, no reservations required. Turn down the lights, put on a jazzy playlist, and have everyone dress up a little as you turn your kitchen into a hotel bar at home.

Checking In!

PUT IT ON THE RITZ

One 1-ounce jar caviar

One 1-ounce jar salmon roe

4 to 6 tablespoons crème fraîche

2 tablespoons chopped fresh chives

1 to 2 sleeves Ritz crackers

SERVES 4

Here is an unpretentious way to serve one of happy hour's most luxe menu items. If you're keen to serve caviar at a get-together, your bougie meter is already off the charts, so give yourself permission to pair the pricey salt-cured roe with something timeless (and cheap)—put it on the Ritz (cracker). Serve with bright and dry Champagne or other sparkling wine.

Select a large serving tray or board. Place two small glass bowls on opposite sides of the tray or board. Fill each bowl with ice chips or crushed ice. Open the caviar and salmon roe containers 15 to 20 minutes before serving and nestle a container in each bowl of ice. (Caviar and salmon roe must be kept cold while serving to ensure good flavor.) Outfit each container with a small nonreactive spoon—wood, mother-of-pearl, horn, or plastic—for serving. Metal spoons will react with the caviar, giving it a strong off-taste.

Spoon the crème fraîche and chives into separate small bowls and add them to the tray or board. Open a sleeve or two of Ritz crackers and place on the tray. Serve at once.

MARTINI

GARLIC-ROSEMARY FRIES WITH PARMESAN

½ bag (14 ounces) frozen French fries

2 tablespoons extra-virgin olive oil

2 tablespoons minced garlic

1 tablespoon minced fresh rosemary leaves

1 teaspoon kosher salt

Freshly ground black pepper

½ cup grated Parmigiano-Reggiano cheese

SERVES 4

There is something so holy about sitting down with your best friend for a steak dinner and sharing a bowl of garlic fries. My oldest and best friend, Alex, and I love a fancy dinner out at Houston's (our fave classic steakhouse). One reason we always return to Houston's is that a waiter brings you a freshly chilled glass halfway through your martini so your cocktail stays perfectly chilled. These punchy garlic fries are exactly what I want to be nibbling on between bites of a medium-rare New York strip.

TO COOK IN AN AIR FRYER, preheat the air fryer to 400°F. You may need to cook the fries in batches, depending on the size of your air fryer, to avoid crowding. Spread the fries in a single layer in the air fryer basket and cook, turning the fries halfway through cooking, for 12 to 14 minutes, or until crispy. If cooking in batches, keep the first batch hot while cooking the second.

TO COOK IN THE OVEN, preheat the oven to 400°F. Spread the fries in a single layer on a large sheet pan (or use two pans) and bake, turning the fries halfway through cooking, for 20 to 25 minutes, or until crispy.

While the fries are cooking, in a small bowl, whisk together the olive oil, garlic, rosemary, salt and a few grinds of pepper.

Pile the hot fries on a platter or in a large bowl. Drizzle the olive oil mixture evenly over the fries, dust evenly with the cheese, and then toss together until the fries are well coated. Serve immediately.

ELIZABETH'S TIP

For ultra-crispy results, I like making these fries in the air fryer.

CRAZY HORSE DAIQUIRI

2 ounces white rum of choice

1 ounce passion fruit liqueur

½ ounce fresh lime juice

½ ounce simple syrup (optional; page 198)

1 passion fruit, halved

2 ounces prosecco, in a shot glass

SERVES 1

A few years ago, while on a quick trip to Paris, Jared and I went to the Crazy Horse de Paris cabaret to see its legendary burlesque-style show. Inspired by that visit, I created this fruity daiquiri, which is a playful spin on the porn star martini, with the vodka swapped out for rum to play up the signature passion fruit flavor. But I kept the best of the porn star: a shot of prosecco served on the side. This theatrical drink will be the climax of your evening. Any mid-tier white rum works well for this recipe.

In a cocktail shaker, combine the rum, passion fruit liqueur, lime juice, and the simple syrup if you like a sweeter cocktail. Using a spoon, scoop the seed-filled pulp from each passion fruit half into the shaker. Reserve an emptied passion fruit half for garnish. Add 2 scoops of ice, cover the shaker, and shake hard for 10 to 15 seconds, or until the outside of the shaker is frosty cold to the touch.

Strain into a chilled coupe (strain carefully to ensure no passion fruit seeds escape into the glass). Garnish with the reserved passion fruit half and serve the shot glass of prosecco on the side.

NEW YORK SIDECAR

2 ounces Cognac

¾ ounce curaçao

½ ounce fresh lemon juice

½ ounce fresh orange juice

¼ to ½ ounce red wine, for floater

Lemon twist, for garnish

SERVES 1

I love a sidecar at a hotel bar. This New York sidecar is the perfect blend of a classic sour cocktail. My take respects the original but adds a red wine floater for an eye-catching, two-toned layered effect that also tempers the sweetness. Any drink with Cognac will have you instantly escaping to somewhere fancy.

In a cocktail shaker, combine the Cognac, curaçao, lemon juice, and orange juice. Add 2 scoops of ice, cover the shaker, and shake hard for 10 to 15 seconds, or until the outside of the shaker is frosty cold to the touch.

Strain into a rocks glass over ice. To float the red wine on top, hold a barspoon, convex side up, just above the surface of the drink and pour the wine in a slow, thin stream onto the spoon. Garnish with the lemon twist.

THE HISTORIC
SHOTGUN
SUITE
New York, NY
9
AMERICAN EXPRESS
23
HALSTEAD
Hand Made
Maison Louis Marie
No.04
Bois de Balincourt
Huile parfumée / Perfume oil
℮ 15 ml – 0.50 fl. oz.
quand la soif devient plaisir...
CAMPARI
l'aperitivo
TOM FORD
SANTAL
BLUSH
EAU DE PARFUM
30 ML

THE GREEN KEY

- 8 ounces water
- 4 ounces fresh lime juice
- 1 cucumber, sliced
- 1 cup loosely packed fresh mint leaves
- 2 ounces agave nectar
- Soda water, for topping
- Cucumber ribbons and fresh mint sprigs, for garnish

SERVES 4

ZERO PROOF 0% ZERO PROOF

Consider this a stolen green key. It's the ideal high-flavor mocktail to prime you for wherever the night might steal you away. It is also an excellent hydrating green cucumber juice blend for sipping while getting ready for the evening ahead. Add 2 ounces tequila or vodka to easily turn this beverage into a cocktail.

In a blender, combine the water, lime juice, cucumber slices, mint, and agave nectar and blend until a smooth, thick liquid forms. Strain through a fine-mesh strainer into a medium pitcher. Cover and refrigerate until well chilled.

Fill four rocks glasses with ice. Divide the mocktail evenly among the glasses, then top each glass with 2 to 3 ounces soda water and stir gently. Garnish each glass with an accordion-folded cucumber ribbon and mint leaf on a cocktail pick.

ELIZABETH'S TIP

For the cucumber ribbons, use a vegetable peeler to cut paper-thin lengthwise ribbons from a cucumber. Fold accordion style and spear with a mint leaf on a cocktail pick.

FRENCH 92

1 ounce gin

½ ounce fresh lemon juice

½ ounce simple syrup (page 198)

4 ounces pink prosecco or Champagne, chilled

Raspberry and lemon peel, for garnish (optional)

SERVES 1

After I have a few of these, it will be the last time you'll see me for the night. The French 92 is the perfect sparkling drink to toast the end of the evening. Top it with pink prosecco (a personal favorite) for an extremely fun color and wonderful taste.

In a mixing glass, combine the gin, lemon juice, and simple syrup. Fill the glass two-thirds full with ice, then, using a barspoon, stir around the edge of the glass twenty to thirty times, or until well chilled.

Strain into a coupe or champagne flute and top with the prosecco. Garnish with the raspberry and lemon peel (if using).

$50 SEAFOOD TOWER

Calabrian Chile Cocktail Sauce (page 181)

Rémoulade (page 205)

Ponzu Mignonette (page 206)

Lemon wedges

2 or 3 frozen lobster tails, about 4 to 5 ounces each

1 pound large shrimp, peeled and deveined with tails intact

8 to 12 oysters, freshly shucked (see Elizabeth's Tip)

8 ounces store-bought crab salad or poke

SERVES 4 TO 6

Chilled, stacked, and dramatic are how I like my seafood towers and my cocktails. If you love to order a stiff dirty martini or a glass of Champagne, there's a good chance you're also after the raw bar or seafood tower. There's no wrong way to build a seafood tower, but there is a cheaper way. This home version spends about forty dollars on seafood, leaving you ten bucks in the budget for sauce ingredients, lemons, and seafood salad.

First, prepare the cocktail sauce, rémoulade, and/or mignonette for serving with the seafood and set them aside in small bowls. Put the lemon wedges into a small bowl and set alongside the sauce.

TO COOK THE LOBSTER, fill a medium pot three-fourths full with salted water and bring to a boil over high heat. Add the lobster tails and cook for 8 to 10 minutes, or until they turn bright red. Remove the tails from the pot and set aside to cool, then cut each tail in half or in quarters.

TO COOK THE SHRIMP, remove the pot of boiling water from the heat, add the shrimp, and cover the pot. Let the shrimp "cook" in the hot water for 3 to 4 minutes, or until they are opaque and pink. Meanwhile, in a large bowl, combine equal parts ice cubes and water.

When the shrimp are ready, using a slotted spoon, transfer them to the ice bath and let cool for 2 to 3 minutes. Then, using the slotted spoon, transfer them to a plate and blot dry with paper towels.

Spoon the crab salad into an attractive small serving bowl.

TO ASSEMBLE THE TOWER, fill the tiers on a two- or three-tiered tower with crushed ice and divide up the seafood on the tiers as you like. For example, arrange the oysters on the half shell on the ice on the bottom tier. Top the remaining tier(s) with the cooked lobster and shrimp. Place the crab salad in a bowl nearby. Arrange the sauces and lemon wedges alongside the tower and outfit each sauce bowl with a small spoon. Serve immediately.

ELIZABETH'S TIP

Order up freshly shucked oysters from your favorite seafood market. (To shuck your own, see page 206.) You can also use pre-cooked shrimp to save time.

SPICY DIRTY MARTINI OLIVES

1 small wedge fresh goat cheese (about 2½ ounces), at room temperature

2 tablespoons gin

One 10-ounce jar pitted large green olives, drained

Grated zest of 1 orange

Grated zest and juice of 1 lemon

½ teaspoon red pepper flakes

2 garlic cloves, minced

1 tablespoon chopped fresh rosemary leaves

4 ounces Gouda cheese, cut into 1-inch cubes

Extra-virgin olive oil, for drizzling

Crackers or baguette slices, for serving as a snack

SERVES 6 AS A SNACK

One of my VIP snacks, these goat cheese–stuffed olives are marinated in a citrusy mixture that is equally savory and spicy. They are the kind of bite that you would be elated to find in a small crystal bowl on top of any hotel bar. Snack on them or skewer them onto a cocktail pick for tipping into a dirty martini.

Put the goat cheese into a small bowl and drizzle the gin over the cheese. Using a fork or the back of a spoon, smash the cheese to a creamy paste. Transfer to a resealable bag, secure the bag closed, and snip off a lower corner.

Pipe the goat cheese mixture into each olive, adding the olives to a medium bowl as you work.

Add the orange zest, lemon zest and juice, pepper flakes, garlic, rosemary, and Gouda cubes to the bowl with the olives. Drizzle with the olive oil, adding just enough to coat the olives and cheese cubes lightly, then toss gently but thoroughly until well coated.

If serving the olives as a snack, accompany them with your favorite crackers or bread slices. If using the olives for garnishing dirty martinis, slide an olive—or 3—onto a cocktail pick and tip the pick into the glass. The olives will keep in an airtight container in the refrigerator for up to 2 weeks.

ELIZABETH'S TIP

If you prefer a blue cheese–stuffed olive, just swap out the goat cheese for a wedge of your favorite blue.

Petites Pommes
· classic floats ·

MINI CALIFORNIA CLUB SANDWICHES

¼ cup mayonnaise

1 tablespoon sriracha sauce

3 slices sourdough bread

Unsalted butter, at room temperature, for spreading

1 romaine lettuce leaf

2 tomato slices

Kosher salt and freshly ground black pepper

2 bacon slices, cooked until crisp

2 slices pepper jack cheese

3 or 4 thin slices deli roast turkey

½ avocado, peeled and sliced

MAKES 1 SANDWICH (4 TRIANGLES)

Here, the classic club sandwich is given a spicy California update. Slices of sourdough spread with sriracha mayonnaise conceal creamy avocado, crisp bacon, deli turkey slices, and buttery, tangy pepper jack. Once you've assembled the sandwich, cut it into four snack-size triangles for easy sharing.

In a small bowl, stir together the mayonnaise and sriracha until well mixed. Set aside.

Toast the bread slices until golden, then spread a thin layer of butter on both sides of each slice.

Spread a thin layer of the sriracha mayonnaise on one side of a toasted bread slice. Top with the lettuce leaf and the tomato slices and season lightly with salt and pepper. Place the bacon pieces on top.

Spread a thin layer of the sriracha mayonnaise on both sides of a second slice of toasted bread and place the bread on top of the bacon layer. Then layer the cheese slices, then the turkey slices, and finally the avocado slices on top. Season the avocado lightly with salt and pepper.

Spread a thin layer of sriracha mayonnaise on one side of the third toasted bread slice and place the slice, mayonnaise side down, on the avocado layer. Secure each corner of the sandwich with a toothpick, then cut into 4 triangles and serve.

Hotel
Rascal

Hawaiian Sun
PASS-O-GUAVA NECTAR
Hawaiian Sun
GREEN TEA
Hawaiian Sun
LILIKOI LYCHEE
JUICE DRINK

Meet Me at the Cabana

BANANA CABANA COLD BREW

¼ banana, peeled

1 ounce banana liqueur

¼ teaspoon ground cinnamon

1 ounce rum of choice

3 ounces cold brew coffee

1 ounce heavy cream or half-and-half

SERVES 1

This coffee cocktail is the tropical, fruity version of an espresso martini. Its tasting notes combine the comforting spice of a slice of cinnamon banana bread and the smoothness of creamy cold brew coffee. This is unquestionably what I want to be sipping in the morning at a beachside cabana.

In a cocktail shaker, combine the banana, banana liqueur, and cinnamon and muddle until the banana is smashed. Add the rum, cold brew, cream, and 2 scoops of ice. Cover the shaker and shake hard for 10 to 15 seconds, or until the outside of the shaker is frosty cold to the touch.

Strain into a tumbler or pint glass over ice.

ELIZABETH'S TIP

I love adding banana liqueur to coffee-based breakfast cocktails and whiskey-based drinks like an old fashioned to introduce an unexpected flavor.

LUKE'S BIG BATCH MOJITOS

40 fresh mint leaves

10 ounces coconut syrup (page 103)

8 ounces fresh lime juice (about 10 limes)

16 ounces white rum

8 cups ice

One 33.8-ounce (1 liter) bottle soda water

2 limes, thinly sliced, and 15 fresh mint leaves, for garnish

SERVES 8

A few summers ago, I brought a big batch of mojitos to my friend Luke's birthday party. I know from experience that when people start asking for the recipe after one or two glasses, you've made something memorable. Luke still loves to make (and drink, ha!) these mojitos, so it's only appropriate that I've named them after him. These are fresh, bubbly, and made with a sweetened coconut syrup that I use in my Fauxjito (page 103) as well.

Put the mint leaves into a drink dispenser or large glass pitcher and muddle until they are aromatic. Add the coconut syrup, lime juice, and rum and stir until well mixed.

Add the ice, then pour in the soda water and stir to mix. Garnish with the lime slices and mint leaves. Serve in collins glasses.

THE FAUXJITO

FOR THE COCONUT SYRUP

8 ounces water

1 cup sugar

½ cup unsweetened dried coconut flakes

FOR THE MOCKTAIL

5 fresh mint leaves

1 ounce coconut syrup

1 ounce fresh lime juice

3 ounces soda water

Lime wheels and fresh mint leaves, for garnish

SERVES 1

ZERO PROOF 0%

Meet The Fauxjito. It has everything you love about a mojito, but it's alcohol-free. To make sure this mocktail has something noteworthy, I created a rich coconut syrup that delivers the essence of rum with 0% ABV. This refined drink is as thoughtful and intentional as any cocktail.

TO MAKE THE COCONUT SYRUP, in a small saucepan, whisk together the water and sugar. Place over medium heat and cook, stirring often, for 4 to 5 minutes, until the sugar is completely dissolved and the liquid is clear. Remove from the heat.

Add the coconut flakes, stir to mix well, and let steep for 15 minutes. For a stronger coconut flavor, let the syrup steep longer. Strain the syrup through a fine-mesh strainer into a glass jar. You should have about 1¼ cups. It will keep tightly capped in the refrigerator for up to 2 weeks.

TO ASSEMBLE THE MOCKTAIL, put the mint leaves into a cocktail shaker and muddle until they are aromatic. Add the coconut syrup, lime juice, and 2 scoops of ice. Cover the shaker and shake hard for 10 to 15 seconds, or until the outside of the shaker is frosty cold to the touch.

Strain into a highball or other tall glass (10 to 12 ounces) over ice. Top with the soda water and stir gently. Garnish with the lime wheels and mint leaves.

POKE TWO WAYS: CITRUSY AND SPICY

FOR THE SPICY POKE

8 ounces sushi-grade ahi tuna fillet, cut into ¼-inch dice

2 tablespoons soy sauce

2 teaspoons toasted sesame oil

2 tablespoons mayonnaise

4 teaspoons sriracha sauce

1 garlic clove, grated

2 green onions, white and green parts, thinly sliced

FOR THE CITRUSY POKE

8 ounces sushi-grade ahi tuna fillet, cut into ¼-inch dice

2 tablespoons soy sauce

1 teaspoon toasted sesame oil

1 tablespoon ponzu sauce (see Elizabeth's Tip, page 206)

Grated zest of 1 lime

2 teaspoons fresh lime juice

1 garlic clove, grated

1 teaspoon grated, peeled fresh ginger

2 green onions, white and green parts, thinly sliced

FOR THE BAKED WONTON CHIPS

Olive oil cooking spray, for the pan and chips

12 refrigerated wonton sheets

Sesame seeds, for sprinkling

SERVES 2 TO 4

There is that moment on any afternoon in a cabana (usually hour three) where you're feeling a little crispy from the sun, a little tipsy from the margaritas, and extremely ready for a snack. You want something fresh and cold but still flavorful and delicious. These citrusy and spicy poke flavors are the ideal cure for your cabana hunger cues. They go together quickly and can be customized to your desired spice level. If you are too hungry to make the wonton chips, tortilla chips are a good stand-in.

TO MAKE THE SPICY POKE, in a medium bowl, combine the tuna, soy sauce, and sesame oil and stir gently until the tuna is evenly coated. Cover and refrigerate for 20 to 30 minutes to marinate.

Add the mayonnaise, sriracha, garlic, and most of the green onions, reserving a little for garnish. Stir gently until the tuna is evenly coated. Cover and refrigerate until serving.

TO MAKE THE CITRUSY POKE, in a medium bowl, combine the tuna, soy sauce, sesame oil, ponzu sauce, lime zest and juice, garlic, ginger, and most of the green onions, reserving a little for garnish. Stir gently until the tuna is evenly coated. Cover and refrigerate for 20 to 30 minutes to marinate.

TO MAKE THE BAKED WONTON CHIPS, while the poke mixtures are marinating, preheat the oven to 400°F. Spray two 9-by-13-inch sheet pans with cooking spray.

Cut each wonton wrapper into 2 triangles. Arrange half of the wonton triangles on each prepared sheet pan, spacing them evenly apart. Spray the tops of the triangles with cooking spray, then sprinkle lightly with sesame seeds.

Bake for 4 to 5 minutes, or until golden and crisp. Let cool completely on the pans on wire racks.

Top the poke with the reserved green onions and serve dip-style with the wonton chips.

KEY LIME PIE MATCHA

FOR THE COCONUT CREAM

2 ounces heavy cream

1 teaspoon sugar

¼ teaspoon coconut extract

FOR THE DRINK

1 teaspoon ceremonial-grade matcha powder

2 ounces room-temperature water

4 ounces limeade

Grated lime zest, for garnish

SERVES 1

ZERO PROOF 0%

If Key lime pie is on a restaurant menu, there is a good chance I'll order it. Here, I've successfully turned one of my favorite desserts into a drink. This icy matcha-based beverage has hints of coconut and lime and serves as a great afternoon refresher with a caffeine kick that won't make you crash.

TO MAKE THE COCONUT CREAM, in a small bowl, combine the cream, sugar, and coconut extract. Using a handheld frother, whip together for 20 to 30 seconds, or until the mixture is light and airy and has the texture of soft whipped cream. Cover and refrigerate until serving.

TO MAKE THE DRINK, in a small bowl, whisk together the matcha and water until the matcha is fully dissolved. (You will get the best results with a matcha whisk, but a small kitchen whisk will also work.)

Fill a collins or other tall glass (10 to 12 ounces) with ice. Pour in the limeade. To float the matcha on top, hold a barspoon, convex side up, just above the surface of the drink and pour the matcha in a slow, thin stream onto the spoon. Top with the coconut cream and a little lime zest.

PASSION FRUIT MARGARITA WITH TROPICAL FOAM

FOR THE PITCHER MARGARITA

8 ounces silver (blanco) tequila

2 ounces orange curaçao

2 ounces fresh lime juice

4 ounces passion fruit juice (see Elizabeth's Tip)

2 ounces agave nectar

FOR THE FOAM

1 egg white

1 ounce simple syrup

1 ounce honey

1 ounce passion fruit juice

Grated lime zest, for garnish (optional)

SERVES 4

FOR A SINGLE MARGARITA

If you prefer to make just one margarita at a time, in a cocktail shaker, combine 2 ounces silver (blanco) tequila, ½ ounce orange curaçao, ½ ounce fresh lime juice, 1 ounce passion fruit juice, and ½ ounce agave nectar. Add 2 scoops of ice, cover the shaker, and shake hard for 10 to 15 seconds, or until the outside of the shaker is frosty cold to the touch. Strain into a rocks glass over ice, top with one-fourth of the foam, and garnish with a little lime zest, if desired.

Ever since my trip to Maui, I had been dreaming of re-creating a cocktail I had at the popular Monkeypod Kitchen restaurant. It was technically a mai tai, but my cocktail repertoire was forever changed by the passion fruit foam that topped the drink. My version is a passion fruit margarita crowned with a silky, tropical passion fruit foam. This drink is a bit challenging to make but 100 percent worth the effort.

TO MAKE THE PITCHER MARGARITA, in a medium pitcher, combine the tequila, curaçao, lime juice, passion fruit juice, and agave nectar and stir vigorously until well mixed. Cover and refrigerate for 1 to 2 hours to chill well.

TO MAKE THE FOAM, just before serving, in a stand mixer fitted with the whisk attachment or in a medium bowl with a handheld mixer, beat together the egg white, simple syrup, honey, and passion fruit juice on high speed for 4 to 6 minutes, or until the foam holds soft peaks.

Fill four rocks glasses with ice and pour in the margarita mix. Top each cocktail with one-fourth of the foam, then garnish with a little lime zest, if desired.

ELIZABETH'S TIP

Want to know one of the strangest (and best) places I use to source fresh produce? Facebook Marketplace! Seriously. People who have a big fruit tree in their backyard are begging to get rid of fruit. Look for fresh passion fruit juice at upscale supermarkets or Asian markets or make your own.

PIERRE
FERRAND
Dry CURAÇAO

COCONUT SHRIMP WITH SRIRACHA DIPPING SAUCE

FOR THE SHRIMP

¼ cup all-purpose flour

1 teaspoon garlic powder

1 teaspoon sweet paprika

1 teaspoon kosher salt

2 eggs

¾ cup unsweetened dried coconut flakes

¾ cup panko bread crumbs

1 pound large shrimp, peeled and deveined with tail segment intact

Olive oil cooking spray, for the pan or basket and shrimp

Olive oil, for drizzling (optional)

FOR THE DIPPING SAUCE

¼ cup sweet chile sauce

¼ cup orange marmalade

1 tablespoon sriracha sauce

1 teaspoon sesame seeds

SERVES 4 TO 6

A basket of crispy coconut shrimp is a cabana staple. Here, I coat succulent shrimp in an aromatic coconut-panko mixture, cook them in an air fryer or the oven—your choice!—and pair them with a spicy sriracha dipping sauce. Serve this crowd favorite with a round of passion fruit margaritas (page 108).

TO MAKE THE SHRIMP, line up three small shallow bowls. In the first bowl, combine the flour, garlic powder, paprika, and salt and mix well. In the second bowl, whisk the eggs until blended. In the third bowl, combine the coconut flakes and panko and mix well.

One at a time, dredge the shrimp in the flour mixture, tapping off the excess, then dip in the egg, allowing the excess to drip off; and finally, coat with the coconut mixture, pressing with your fingertips so it adheres. As each shrimp is ready, set aside on a large plate.

TO COOK IN THE OVEN, preheat the oven to 425°F. Spray a large sheet pan with cooking spray. Arrange the shrimp on the prepared pan, spacing them evenly. Spray the shrimp with cooking spray or drizzle with olive oil.

Bake the shrimp for 9 to 10 minutes, or until the tops are golden and the shrimp are opaque in the center when tested with a knife tip.

TO COOK IN AN AIR FRYER, preheat the air fryer to 400°F. Spray the bottom of the air fryer basket with cooking spray. You may need to cook the shrimp in two batches, depending on the size of your air fryer. Place the shrimp in a single layer in the basket, spacing them about ½ inch apart. Spray the shrimp with cooking spray or drizzle with olive oil. Cook the shrimp for 4 minutes, flip them, and continue cooking until the tops are golden and the shrimp are opaque in the center when tested with a knife tip. (If cooking in batches, keep the first batch warm while cooking the second batch.)

TO MAKE THE DIPPING SAUCE, while the shrimp are cooking, in a small bowl, combine the chile sauce, marmalade, sriracha, and sesame seeds and stir until well mixed and smooth.

Arrange the shrimp on a platter and serve hot with the dipping sauce alongside.

POGMOSA

3 ounces store-bought POG juice, chilled (see Elizabeth's Tip)

5 ounces Champagne or prosecco, chilled

SERVES 1

This cocktail instantly transports me to a Hawaiian Airlines flight, which is somewhere I always want to be! POG is a tropical juice blend of passion fruit, orange, and guava coined by Hawaiian locals. Mix POG with Champagne and you have a great mimosa that will have you dreaming of swaying palm trees and white sand beaches.

Add the POG juice to a champagne flute or wineglass. Top with the Champagne.

POG FIZZ

2 ounces POG juice, chilled (see Elizabeth's Tip)

4 ounces club soda or ginger beer, chilled

SERVES 1

ZERO PROOF 0% ZERO PROOF

POG juice is the perfect base for a nonalcoholic mimosa-like fizzy beverage. Here, its bold, fruity flavors shine through when topped with club soda or ginger beer, but it would be good with a nonalcoholic prosecco too.

Add the POG juice to a champagne flute or wineglass. Top with the club soda.

ELIZABETH'S TIP

POG juice can be hard to find on the mainland, with stores on the West Coast the best bet. If you come up empty handed, you can create a respectable substitute by mixing equal parts of the three juices, then adjusting the blend to suit your taste.

PINEAPPLE COCONUT LOAF CAKE

FOR THE CAKE

½ cup (1 stick) unsalted butter, at room temperature, plus more for the pan

1½ cups all-purpose flour, plus more for the pan

1½ cups sweetened shredded dried coconut

½ teaspoon baking soda

½ teaspoon kosher salt

1 cup granulated sugar

3 eggs

1 teaspoon coconut extract

1 cup sour cream

1½ cups finely diced fresh pineapple

½ cup chopped macadamia nuts (optional)

FOR THE GLAZE

⅔ cup powdered sugar

3 tablespoons pineapple juice

¼ teaspoon coconut extract

SERVES 8 TO 10

Some of my most significant stops in Hawaii were at the stands selling fresh pineapple juice and banana bread on the side of the road. Jared and I would make a stop at one or the other daily and take a treat back to the pool or beach. I created this loaf cake to celebrate that roadside tradition.

TO MAKE THE CAKE, preheat the oven to 350°F. Butter a 9-by-5-inch loaf pan, then dust with flour, tapping out the excess.

Spread 1 cup of the shredded coconut on a small sheet pan. Toast, tossing halfway through, until lightly golden and fragrant, about 8 minutes. Let cool. Reserve the remaining ½ cup for the top of the cake.

In a medium bowl, whisk together the flour, baking soda, and salt. In a stand mixer fitted with the paddle attachment, or using a handheld mixer, beat the butter and granulated sugar on medium-high speed until pale and fluffy, 2 to 3 minutes. Scrape down the sides of the bowl. On medium speed, add the eggs one at a time, beating well after each addition. Add the coconut extract with the final egg.

On medium-low speed, add the flour mixture in three batches alternating with the sour cream in two batches, beginning and ending with the flour. Beat after each addition just until incorporated. Turn off the mixer. Fold in the pineapple, macadamia nuts (if using), and 1 cup toasted coconut with a rubber spatula until just combined.

Pour the batter into the prepared pan and sprinkle the remaining ½ cup untoasted coconut evenly on top. Bake for 40 minutes, then loosely tent the top with foil to prevent overbrowning. Continue baking for 25 to 30 minutes more, or until a toothpick inserted in the center comes out clean. Cool in the pan on a wire rack for 30 to 40 minutes, then unmold, turn right side up, and cool completely.

TO MAKE THE GLAZE, in a small bowl, whisk together the powdered sugar, pineapple juice, and coconut extract until smooth.

When the cake has cooled, transfer it to a serving plate and drizzle the glaze evenly over the top. Let it sit just until the glaze sets, then serve. Aloha!

LOTERIA
TABLA 6
LOTERIA
Topo Chico

Salud

HECHO E
A BLEND OF H
SUSTAINABL
SUN
Teq
B L A
DENOMINACIÓN DE O

HIBISCUS MEZCAL

FOR THE HIBISCUS SYRUP

1 cup water

1 cup sugar

1 cup dried hibiscus flowers

FOR THE COCKTAIL

2 ounces mezcal

1 ounce Cointreau or other orange liqueur

1 ounce fresh lime juice

1 ounce hibiscus syrup

Fresh hibiscus flower or lime wheel, for garnish

SERVES 1

She's sweet, sexy, and bold. Heady with hibiscus, this mezcal-based cocktail is everything you love in an old fashioned and a margarita in a single coupe. Each sip has a bit of a smoky undertone from the mezcal and a sweet floral note from the homemade hibiscus syrup. The syrup is easy to make and will impart a vibrant, rich color to cocktails or batches of lemonade or can be drizzled over ice cream or other sweet treats. Look for dried hibiscus flowers in herb shops, natural foods stores, well-stocked supermarkets, Mexican markets (where they are labeled *flor de jamaica*), or online.

TO MAKE THE HIBISCUS SYRUP, in a small saucepan over medium heat, whisk together the water and sugar for 4 to 5 minutes, or until the sugar is fully dissolved and the mixture is clear. Remove from the heat.

Add the dried hibiscus flowers, stir briefly, and then let the syrup steep for 10 to 15 minutes. Strain the syrup through a fine-mesh strainer into a glass jar and discard the spent flowers. Let cool completely, then cap tightly and store in the refrigerator for up to 2 weeks.

TO MAKE THE COCKTAIL, in a cocktail shaker, combine the mezcal, Cointreau, lime juice, and hibiscus syrup. Add 2 scoops of ice, cover the shaker, and shake hard for 10 to 15 seconds, or until the outside of the shaker is frosty cold to the touch.

Strain into a coupe glass and garnish with the fresh hibiscus flower.

ELIZABETH'S TIP

Add 1 to 2 ounces hibiscus syrup to a tall glass of chilled Topo Chico for an easy and inventive NA beverage.

ORIGINAL

AHI TUNA AND MANGO TOSTADAS

FOR THE TUNA

8 ounces sushi-grade ahi tuna fillet, cut into ¼-inch dice

3 tablespoons soy sauce

1 tablespoon fresh lime juice

FOR THE SPICY MAYONNAISE

¼ cup mayonnaise

2 teaspoons sriracha sauce

2 teaspoons Asian sesame oil

2 teaspoons agave nectar

FOR THE TOSTADAS

4 to 6 corn tostada shells, each about 6 inches in diameter

1 avocado, halved, pitted, peeled, and diced

½ cup diced mango

Chopped green onions, white and green parts, for garnish

Fresh cilantro leaves, for garnish

Sesame seeds, for garnish

1 jalapeño chile, thinly sliced, for garnish

Lime wedges, for serving

SERVES 4 TO 6

I went on a girls' trip to Spain a few years ago, and one thing was certain, we were stopping for tapas every day. Sipping a glass of cava and trying a new tapa at three o'clock in the afternoon was my favorite part of each day. The tapa that stands out the most from that trip was a tuna and mango tostada. It had pieces of luscious ahi, silky avocado, and juicy mango. On top was a creamy, spicy mayonnaise and fresh herbs. This is my version, and I think you'll love it as much as I loved the Spanish original. Don't forget the cava!

TO PREPARE THE TUNA, in a medium bowl, combine the tuna, soy sauce, and lime juice and toss together until the tuna is evenly coated. Cover and refrigerate for at least 30 minutes or up to 2 hours before serving.

TO MAKE THE SPICY MAYONNAISE, in a small bowl, stir together the mayonnaise, sriracha, sesame oil, and agave nectar until well mixed and creamy. Transfer to a resealable bag, secure closed, and refrigerate until serving.

TO ASSEMBLE THE TOSTADAS, scoop the tuna onto the tostada shells, dividing it evenly. Snip a lower corner off the bag holding the spicy mayonnaise and pipe small dollops of the mayonnaise onto the tuna. Top with the avocado and mango, dividing them evenly, then garnish with the green onions, cilantro, sesame seeds, and chile slices. Arrange on a platter and serve at once.

SQUIRT PALOMA

Tajín, grated lime zest, and lime wedge, for rimming the glass

2 ounces silver (blanco) tequila

2 ounces fresh grapefruit juice

1 ounce fresh lime juice

3 to 4 ounces Squirt or other grapefruit soda, chilled

Grapefruit wedges, for garnish

SERVES 1

Did you have Squirt soda as a kid? I grew up with a mom who had a two-liter bottle of the citrusy soda in our fridge at all times. Loaded with grapefruit notes, it tasted more like juice than its lemon-lime soda competition. I like pairing it with tequila for a fun twist on the paloma. Serve it with Mini Cheese-Crusted Chipotle Chicken Quesadillas (page 129) for a happy hour, Mexican-style. *¡Salud!*

Mix a thin layer of Tajín and lime zest on a flat saucer. Rub the outside rim of a tall glass with the lime wedge, then holding the glass at an angle almost parallel to the saucer, roll the dampened edge in the Tajín mixture to coat lightly. Set the glass aside.

In a cocktail shaker, combine the tequila, grapefruit juice, and lime juice. Add 2 scoops of ice, cover the shaker, and shake hard for 10 to 15 seconds, or until the outside of the shaker is frosty cold to the touch.

Fill the Tajín-rimmed glass with ice, then strain the contents of the shaker into the glass. Top with the Squirt, stir gently, and garnish with the grapefruit wedges.

Squirt

MEXICAN SUERO

Tajín and lime wedge, for rimming the glass

Juice of 1 lime

Generous pinch of kosher salt

Topo Chico or other sparkling mineral water, chilled, for topping

Lime wedge, for garnish

SERVES 1

My friend Abbie came back from a trip to Mexico and raved about the suero, a hydrating drink that is not only refreshing but also a great hangover remedy. It's basically Topo Chico (extra-bubbly mineral water from Monterrey, Mexico) with salt and lime. The first time she made one for me, I realized just how rejuvenating it was. The salt helps your body absorb water more efficiently, and the Topo Chico is great for minerals and hydration.

Pour a thin layer of Tajín onto a flat saucer. Dampen the outside rim of a rocks glass with the lime wedge, then holding the glass at an angle almost parallel to the saucer, roll the dampened edge in the Tajín to coat lightly.

Fill the Tajín-rimmed glass with ice. Add the lime juice and salt, then top with the sparkling water and stir gently. Garnish with the lime wedge.

TABLA 6
LA LUNA
EL COTORRO
LOTERIA
Topo Chico
LA SIRENA

MINI CHEESE-CRUSTED CHIPOTLE CHICKEN QUESADILLAS

FOR THE CHIPOTLE DRIZZLE

½ cup mayonnaise

3 tablespoons adobo sauce from canned chipotle chiles

2 teaspoons fresh lime juice

1 teaspoon honey

1 teaspoon garlic powder

FOR THE QUESADILLAS

3 cups shredded Monterey Jack cheese

6 small flour tortillas, each 6 inches in diameter

1½ cups shredded cooked chicken

Guacamole and sour cream, for serving

SERVES 6

Somehow, nearly everything is cuter and more appetizing in mini form. These cheese-crusted quesadillas are small but mighty. After your first bite, with its smoky kick, melty cheese, and zesty chipotle drizzle, you will see how "roll your eyes amazing" they are. Reach for a refreshing Squirt Paloma (page 124) to wash them down.

TO MAKE THE CHIPOTLE DRIZZLE, in a small bowl, stir together the mayonnaise, adobo sauce, lime juice, honey, and garlic powder, mixing well. Set aside.

TO MAKE THE QUESADILLAS, place a small nonstick skillet over medium heat. Sprinkle ¼ cup of the cheese into the skillet, spreading it evenly in the shape and size of a tortilla. Immediately lay a tortilla on top of the cheese circle.

Sprinkle another ¼ cup of the cheese on the top of the tortilla, spreading it evenly to the edges. Spoon ¼ cup of the chicken onto one side of the tortilla and top the chicken generously with some of the chipotle drizzle.

Once the cheese on the uncovered side of the tortilla has browned, fold the uncovered side over the chicken. Turn the heat down to low and cook for 1 to 2 minutes, or just until the cheese inside the quesadilla is melted. Using a spatula, carefully flip the quesadilla over and cook until the second side is crispy and golden. Transfer to a serving platter and repeat with the remaining cheese, tortillas, and chicken.

Serve the quesadillas hot, finished with more chipotle drizzle, if desired, and accompanied with guacamole and sour cream for topping.

ELIZABETH'S TIP

If you have a large nonstick stovetop griddle, use it for these quesadillas. That way you'll be able to cook two at a time and everyone will be enjoying them sooner.

SWEET AND SPICY WATERMELON SHOTS

Chamoy sauce and Tajín, for rimming the glasses

6 ounces silver (blanco) tequila

2 ounces watermelon juice

1 ounce fresh lime juice

1 ounce chamoy sauce

SERVES 4

There is something wonderful about sitting down on a patio with a couple of girlfriends and a batch of warm tortilla chips, salsa, and guac. If the sun is out, there's a good chance I'm ordering a minimum of three skinny margaritas and a round of these fruit-forward sweet and spicy shots for everyone. Yes, they go down super easily, and I promise you that you and your friends will be wildly praising them rather than reaching for a Pepcid.

Pour a small amount of chamoy sauce onto a flat saucer. Pour a thin layer of Tajín onto a second flat saucer. Holding a shot glass at an angle almost parallel to the saucer with the chamoy, run the edge of the glass through the chamoy, dampening it evenly. Now holding the glass at an angle almost parallel to the saucer with the Tajín, roll the dampened edge in the Tajín to coat lightly. Set the glass aside and rim three more shot glasses the same way.

In a cocktail shaker, combine the tequila, watermelon juice, lime juice, and chamoy and whisk together until well mixed and the chamoy is fully incorporated. Add 2 scoops of ice, cover the shaker, and shake hard for 10 to 15 seconds, or until the outside of the shaker is frosty cold to the touch.

Strain into the Tajín-rimmed shot glasses.

HECHO
A BLEND OF
SUSTAINABL
SUN
Teq
100% AGAVE AZUL
DENOMINACIÓN DE
750ML

HEIDSIECK

Girls' Night Out

SPICY TAMARINDO
GM
EL ÚNICO
GRAN MALO
LIQUEUR
MADE WITH TEQUILA BLANCO AND SUGARCANE SPIRIT
NET. 750 ML
Product of France
Fresh Drawer
HERBY

PINEAPPLE MALO COOLER

Tajín and lime wedge, for rimming the glass

1 ounce Gran Malo spicy tamarindo liqueur

1 ounce silver (blanco) tequila

½ ounce fresh lime juice

1 ounce pineapple juice

Pineapple wedge, for garnish

SERVES 1

FOR PINEAPPLE MALO SHOTS

Rim four shot glasses with Tajín as directed for the rocks glass. In a cocktail shaker, combine 2 ounces Gran Malo spicy tamarindo liqueur, 2 ounces silver (blanco) tequila, 1 ounce fresh lime juice, and 1 ounce pineapple juice. Add 2 scoops of ice, cover the shaker, and shake hard for 10 to 15 seconds, or until the outside of the shaker is frosty cold to the touch. Strain into the four Tajín-rimmed shot glasses and garnish with lime wedges.

I can confidently say that this is currently one of the signature sips of girls' nights. Pineapple is usually a safe flavor bet, and when it's paired with Gran Malo, the girls go absolutely feral. A tamarind liqueur (made with tequila), Gran Malo is dangerously smooth and flavorful. It's great in this icy beverage, or you can turn the same combo into fun fruity shots to get the night started.

Pour a thin layer of Tajín onto a flat saucer. Rub the outside rim of a cocktail glass with the lime wedge, then holding the glass at an angle almost parallel to the saucer, roll the dampened edge in the Tajín to coat lightly. Set the glass aside.

In a cocktail shaker, combine the tamarindo liqueur, tequila, lime juice, and pineapple juice. Add 2 scoops of ice, cover the shaker, and shake hard for 10 to 15 seconds, or until the outside of the shaker is frosty cold to the touch.

Fill the Tajín-rimmed glass with crushed ice and strain the cocktail into the glass. Garnish with the pineapple wedge.

ELIZABETH'S TIP

If you can't find Gran Malo, substitute a flavored tequila.

HOT HONEY PEPPERONI PIZZA

All-purpose flour, for the pan and work surface

1 pound pizza dough (homemade or store-bought)

½ cup store-bought red pizza sauce

2 cups shredded mozzarella cheese

20 slices pepperoni

⅓ cup whole-milk ricotta cheese

1 teaspoon Italian seasoning

1 teaspoon red pepper flakes

Olive oil, for brushing

1 jalapeño chile, stemmed and thinly sliced

Fresh basil leaves, for topping

Hot honey, for drizzling

SERVES 4 TO 6

Digging into a hot pizza and a bottle of cheap rosé can be the foundation for some of the best venting sessions. This seriously cheese-crusted pizza is perfect for serving at the beginning or at the end of the night. It's got just the right amount of sweet and spice to "hit the spot" on either side of an evening. If you have a pizza stone, use it, as it produces a crispier, more evenly cooked crust.

Preheat the oven to 475°F. Lightly dust a large sheet pan with flour.

On a lightly floured work surface, roll out the dough into a round 12 inches in diameter and ¼ inch thick. Transfer the dough round to the prepared sheet pan.

Using the back of a spoon, spread the pizza sauce over the dough round, leaving a 1-inch border free of sauce. Sprinkle 1 cup of the mozzarella evenly over the sauce. Arrange the pepperoni slices in a single layer on the mozzarella and then dollop the ricotta uniformly on top. Sprinkle the pizza evenly with the Italian seasoning and pepper flakes. Brush the edge of the crust with olive oil, then sprinkle the remaining 1 cup mozzarella evenly over the pizza.

Bake for 12 to 15 minutes, or until the edge of the crust is golden brown and the cheese is melted and bubbly.

Let the pizza cool for a few minutes, then top with the jalapeño slices and basil leaves. Finish with a drizzle of hot honey, cut into slices, and serve.

diet

NUTELLA ESPRESSO MARTINI

1 tablespoon Nutella

1 ounce freshly brewed espresso (see Elizabeth's Tip)

2 ounces vodka

1 ounce Kahlúa or other coffee liqueur

½ ounce simple syrup (page 198)

Espresso beans and cocoa powder, for garnish

SERVES 1

Every friend group chat has that one unforgettable night—the kind that you can reference with just an emoji or two and everyone chuckles to themselves. The espresso martini has become that symbol for us. This chocolaty Nutella version is much like the friend who inspired the story: sweet and unforgettable. If you have more than two, I must warn you that your bathroom fixtures may not be safe, but that's one secret we'll never tell. ;)

Add Nutella to the bottom of a shot glass. Brew the espresso directly into the shot glass on top of the Nutella to ensure the Nutella melts. Stir together until creamy and let cool.

In a cocktail shaker, combine the espresso mixture, vodka, Kahlúa, and simple syrup, cover, and dry shake hard for 10 seconds. (This dry shake will help create a foamy top.) Uncover, add 2 scoops of ice, re-cover, and shake hard for 10 to 15 seconds, or until the outside of the shaker is frosty cold to the touch.

Double strain into a chilled martini glass using a fine-mesh strainer along with a Hawthorne strainer (a traditional bar tool with a handle, a perforated metal screen, and a spring fixed around the screen that secures it to the glass to ensure no ice or other bits escape into the cocktail). Garnish with a few espresso beans and a dusting of cocoa powder.

ELIZABETH'S TIP

If you don't have an espresso machine, you can substitute 1 ounce strong cold brew concentrate and omit the simple syrup. Whisk together the cold brew and Nutella until creamy.

GREEN CHILE AND SPINACH ARTICHOKE DIP

- Unsalted butter or nonstick cooking spray, for the baking dish
- One 8-ounce package cream cheese, at room temperature
- ½ cup mayonnaise
- ½ cup sour cream
- 1 cup shredded Parmigiano-Reggiano cheese
- 1 cup shredded mozzarella cheese
- 3 garlic cloves, minced
- One 14-ounce can artichoke hearts in water, drained and finely chopped
- ½ cup thawed and well-drained frozen chopped spinach
- One 4-ounce can diced mild green chiles, drained
- 1 small jalapeño chile, stemmed and finely chopped, plus jalapeño slices for garnish (optional)
- 1 teaspoon kosher salt
- Freshly ground black pepper
- Tortilla chips, crackers, or raw carrot and celery sticks, for serving

SERVES 6

A few years ago, I had a martini-themed dinner party, and I made a really tasty spinach and artichoke dip to pair with the drinks. When I tell you that I had never seen the girls go in so hard on an appetizer as they did this dip, I mean it. It was literally *gone* within minutes. The secret ingredient is the small can of flavor-packed green chiles. They give this creamy classic a new depth of richness and savory flavor.

Preheat the oven to 375°F. Butter a 1-quart baking dish or spray with cooking spray.

In a large bowl, combine the cream cheese, mayonnaise, sour cream, ½ cup of the Parmigiano-Reggiano, ¾ cup of the mozzarella, and the garlic and stir until all the ingredients are evenly distributed and the mixture is smooth. (If the cream cheese isn't at room temperature, you'll need to apply a bit of elbow grease.)

Add the artichokes, spinach, canned chiles, jalapeño, salt, and a few grinds of pepper and stir and toss together just until evenly mixed.

Transfer the artichoke mixture to the prepared baking dish and spread in an even layer. Top evenly with the remaining ½ cup Parmigiano-Reggiano and ¼ cup mozzarella. Bake for 25 to 30 minutes, or until the mixture is bubbling and golden on top.

Remove from the oven and garnish with the jalapeño slices, if desired. Serve warm with tortilla chips.

ELIZABETH'S TIP

You can make this dip the morning or even the night before you plan to serve it, cover and refrigerate it, and then pop it into the oven right before your guests arrive.

THE VOGUE

1½ ounces vodka

½ ounce Cointreau or other orange liqueur

½ ounce pomegranate juice

½ ounce fresh lime juice

Lime twist, for garnish

SERVES 1

I couldn't help but wonder, "Would Carrie Bradshaw be sipping from this martini glass while getting ready for a night out with the girls?" The Vogue is a fresh take on the cosmopolitan—bright from the pomegranate juice, strong from the vodka, and very *feminine*. While you're curling your hair and waiting for your Uber to arrive, you may catch yourself asking, "Was the cosmo my past and the Vogue is my future?"

In a cocktail shaker, combine the vodka, Cointreau, pomegranate juice, and lime juice. Add 2 scoops of ice, cover the shaker, and shake hard for 10 to 15 seconds, or until the outside of the shaker is frosty cold to the touch.

Strain into a chilled coupe or martini glass. Garnish with the lime twist.

NOT-SO-DIRTY SHIRLEY

½ ounce grenadine

1 ounce pomegranate juice

4 to 5 ounces Sprite or other lemon-lime soda, chilled

Maraschino cherries, for garnish

SERVES 1

ZERO PROOF 0%

The Shirley Temple is the most iconic mocktail of all time. Whether you're a kid in a red vinyl restaurant booth or want a drink disguised as a cocktail, the Shirley Temple is there for you. While I love a Dirty Shirley (with vodka), this not-so-dirty version is great to make with lemon-lime soda like Olipop or Poppi! Not only will it taste wonderful, but you'll get great gut health benefits from the prebiotic soda.

Fill a collins glass with ice. Add the grenadine and pomegranate juice, top with the Sprite, and stir gently. Garnish with a few maraschino cherries.

ELIZABETH'S TIP

To make this into a cocktail, add 1½ to 2 ounces vodka.

CHAMPAGNE JELL-O COUPE TOWER

8 ounces water

1 cup sugar

6 teaspoons (3 envelopes) unflavored gelatin powder

16 ounces Champagne, prosecco, or other white sparkling wine

8 ounces vodka

2 ounces fresh lemon juice

6 to 8 maraschino cherries with stems

SERVES 6 TO 8

If you're a girl who loves bottomless Champagne, this one's for you. Glittery and showstopping, this Champagne Jell-O tower is what you want to make for a friend's birthday or a night of celebrating. Each Jell-O coupe is the perfect expression of ice-cold glass of Champagne meets smooth Jell-O shot. It is truly the ultimate party trick.

Measure the 8 ounces water in a measuring cup and sprinkle the gelatin lightly and evenly on top of the water. Allow the gelatin to "bloom" (the granules will visibly swell) for 5 to 10 minutes. This "blooming" step ensures a silky Jell-O texture.

Pour the water-gelatin mixture into a small saucepan and place over medium-low heat. Once the mixture is warm, slowly whisk in the sugar and continue to whisk over medium-low heat just until the sugar is fully dissolved. Set aside for 5 to 10 minutes to cool slightly.

Add the Champagne, vodka, and lemon juice to a large glass measuring pitcher with a spout. Slowly pour the gelatin-sugar mixture into the Champagne mixture while stirring constantly to mix well.

Pour the Champagne mixture into six to eight champagne coupes, dividing it evenly. Add 2 or 3 cherries to each glass. Arrange the glasses on a tray, cover, and refrigerate for at least 4 to 6 hours or up to overnight to set fully.

Arrange the coupes in a champagne tower and serve with small spoons.

GOLDEN GIRL ELIXIR

FOR THE HONEY TURMERIC SYRUP

4 ounces honey

4 ounces water

1 tablespoon turmeric

1 tablespoon ground ginger

1 teaspoon freshly ground black pepper

FOR THE ELIXIR

2 ounces tart cherry or unsweetened pure cranberry juice

1 ounce honey turmeric syrup

½ ounce pineapple juice

½ ounce fresh orange juice

Freshly cracked black pepper, for garnish

Dehydrated orange wheel, for garnish (optional)

SERVES 1

ZERO PROOF 0%

Is it a potion or is it a drink? I'll let you decide. Made with an anti-inflammatory honey turmeric syrup, tart cherry juice for extra melatonin before bed (zzzz), and pineapple for fresh, bold flavor, this beverage has so much goodness that you'll feel like you're sipping on a wellness retreat.

TO MAKE THE HONEY TURMERIC SYRUP, in a small saucepan over medium heat, stir together the honey, water, turmeric, ginger, and pepper and bring to a gentle simmer. Cook, stirring occasionally, for 5 to 10 minutes, or until the honey is fully dissolved. Remove from the heat and let cool to room temperature. Transfer to a glass jar, cap tightly, and store in the refrigerator for up to 2 weeks.

TO MAKE THE ELIXIR, in a cocktail shaker, combine the cherry juice, honey-turmeric syrup, pineapple juice, and orange juice. Add 2 scoops of ice, cover the shaker, and shake hard for 10 to 15 seconds, or until the outside of the shaker is frosty cold to the touch.

Strain into a coupe. Garnish the foam with a very light grind of pepper and the orange wheel (if using).

ELIZABETH'S TIP

To turn the elixir into a cocktail, add 1½ ounces mezcal or gin.

VB
Borgosole

Glow Hour

CITRUS SALMON CRUDO WITH HERBY GREEN SAUCE

6 to 8 ounces sushi-grade salmon fillet, skin removed

FOR THE SAUCE

Leaves from ½ bunch fresh cilantro

Grated zest and juice of ½ lime

Grated zest and juice of ½ orange

1 teaspoon grated, peeled fresh ginger (from about ½-inch piece)

1 heaping tablespoon white miso

2 tablespoons coconut milk

Chile oil, for topping

¼ jalapeño chile, thinly sliced

Fresh micro herbs, such as cilantro, dill, or Thai basil, for topping

Sesame seeds, for sprinkling (optional)

SERVES 4

This dish of raw salmon served atop a bold and herbaceous sauce and finished with fresh chile slices and chile oil may be both the most delicate and the most flavorful recipe in this book. Serving crudo at home is so impressive and yet so simple. My two best tips for success are to use the finest sushi-grade salmon you can source and to chill your serving platter before plating. Keeping your ingredients and serving platter ice-cold is key to serving a restaurant-quality dish at home.

Place a small serving platter or shallow serving bowl in the refrigerator to chill.

Using a long, sharp knife, and holding it at a 30-degree angle, cut the salmon against the grain into pieces ⅛ inch thick and about 1 inch square. Lay the salmon slices on a plate, cover with plastic wrap, and refrigerate until chilled.

TO MAKE THE SAUCE, in a food processor, combine the cilantro, lime zest and juice, orange zest and juice, ginger, miso, and coconut milk and process until very smooth. Strain the sauce through a fine-mesh strainer into a measuring cup with a spout. Cover and refrigerate until well chilled.

To serve, remove the chilled platter or bowl from the refrigerator and drizzle the chilled sauce evenly over the bottom. Lay the salmon slices on the sauce, arranging them in two or three rows and overlapping the slices. Top the sauce with a few dots of chile oil and the salmon with the jalapeño slices and micro herbs. Sprinkle with sesame seeds, if desired, and serve.

YUZU MATCHA SHOTS

¾ teaspoon ceremonial-grade matcha powder

1 ounce hot water

1 ounce honey

2 ounces bottled yuzu juice (I like Yuzuco brand)

SERVES 4

ZERO PROOF 0%

A tasty shot without alcohol? Yes, you read that correctly! The mocktail world has expanded greatly in the last year, but there still aren't a lot of fun NA shot options to choose from—until now. While these citrusy matcha shots may not have alcohol, they do have a little caffeine kick from the matcha and an exotic taste from the yuzu juice. Serve them to kickstart any party.

In a small bowl, whisk together the matcha and hot water until the matcha is fully dissolved. Add the honey and whisk until dissolved.

In a cocktail shaker, combine the matcha mixture and yuzu juice. Add 2 scoops of ice, cover the shaker, and shake hard for 10 to 15 seconds, or until the outside of the shaker is frosty cold to the touch.

Strain into 4 shot glasses.

CRISPY CUCUMBER BITES

24 cucumber slices

½ cup whipped cream cheese, at room temperature

1 tablespoon chopped fresh dill

Pinch of kosher salt

24 small pieces smoked salmon, each about 1-inch square

2 tablespoons chopped fresh chives

Everything bagel seasoning, for sprinkling

1 small jalapeño chile, thinly sliced

MAKES 24 PIECES

You'll catch me ordering spicy tuna crispy rice for the table whenever I go out with friends for sushi. It's one of my favorite appetizers, though I sometimes wish it were a little lighter. These cucumber bites have the same layered vibe and flavors and are great for when you want a snack that has fewer carbs but is still full of flavor.

Arrange the cucumber slices in a single layer on a large plate or platter.

In a medium bowl, combine the cream cheese, dill, and salt and stir until well mixed. Transfer to a piping bag fitted with a ½-inch round or star tip or to a resealable bag, secure the bag closed, and snip off a lower corner with scissors.

Pipe a small dollop of the cream cheese mixture onto the center of each cucumber slice. Top each cream cheese dollop with a piece of smoked salmon, a sprinkle of chives, a sprinkle of everything bagel seasoning and a jalapeño slice. Serve right away.

SPICY JALAPEÑO HUMMUS BOARD

FOR THE TOPPER

2 jalapeño chiles, stemmed and seeded

Leaves from 1 bunch fresh cilantro

Juice of 1 lime

¼ teaspoon ground cumin

¼ teaspoon ground coriander

½ cup olive oil

Kosher salt

One 10-ounce container favorite store-bought hummus

Crackers and raw vegetables, such as carrot and celery sticks, bell pepper strips, cherry tomatoes, cauliflower florets, radishes, and cucumber slices, for serving

SERVES 4 TO 6

If you love to make a charcuterie board for at-home happy hours but want to create something a little lighter, try this fun jalapeño hummus board! Your favorite store-bought hummus is crowned with a zippy and herby jalapeño topper that not only tastes amazing but also looks fancy. Serve it with fresh vegetables and pita wedges or crackers.

TO MAKE THE TOPPER, in a food processor, combine the jalapeños, half of the cilantro, and the lime juice, cumin, coriander, and olive oil and process until the chiles and cilantro are mostly chopped. Add the remaining cilantro and process until chopped. Season with salt.

Spoon the hummus onto a medium serving plate and spread in a shallow circle. Top with the herby jalapeño topper and serve with crackers and vegetables.

ZESTY SKINNY MARGARITA

Pink Himalayan salt and lime wedge, for rimming the glass

2 ounces blanco tequila

1 ounce fresh lime juice

½ ounce fresh orange juice

1 teaspoon agave nectar

Lime wheel and grated lime and/or orange zest, for garnish

SERVES 1

Would you believe me if I told you my first margarita was at Red Lobster? That's weird, I know. I've come a *long* way on my margarita journey since then and consider myself quite a marg connoisseur nowadays. But there is one thing for certain, the skinny margarita is my favorite. You won't find any bottled mixes or refined sweeteners in my shaker. This skinny marg is fresh, zesty, and perfect for any occasion.

Pour a thin layer of Himalayan salt onto a flat saucer. Rub the outside rim of a rocks glass with the lime wedge, then holding the glass at an angle almost parallel to the saucer, roll the dampened edge in the salt to coat lightly. Set the glass aside.

In a cocktail shaker, combine the tequila, lime juice, orange juice, and agave nectar. Add 2 scoops of ice, cover the shaker, and shake hard for 10 to 15 seconds, or until the outside of the shaker is frosty cold to the touch.

Fill the salt-rimmed glass with ice and strain the cocktail into the glass. Garnish with the lime wheel and a little lime and/or orange zest.

ELIZABETH'S TIP

Sometimes I like to muddle a couple of jalapeño slices in the shaker for a spicy flavor.

SIERRA'S AGAVE LIME FRUIT SALAD

2 cups chopped pineapple, in 1-inch pieces

2 cups chopped watermelon, in 1-inch pieces

2 cups chopped honeydew melon, in 1-inch pieces

1 cup chopped mango, in 1-inch pieces

1 cup chopped fresh coconut meat, in 1-inch pieces (see Elizabeth's Tip)

Grated zest and juice of 2 limes, plus more juice for finishing

1½ tablespoons agave nectar

¼ cup finely chopped fresh mint, plus more for garnish

2 cups raspberries (1 pint)

SERVES 6

I know what you're thinking . . . a fruit salad recipe? Yes, fruit salad. But this isn't just any fruit salad. This has become a staple on our house menu. I started making it for my friend Sierra whenever she came over. She always inspires me to eat a little fresher, and she's the epitome of glow hour. I've packed this salad bowl with a nice variety of fruits—cut on the smaller side—and I drizzle them with fresh lime and agave nectar. The secret ingredient, and what makes this salad Sierra's favorite, is fresh coconut chunks. They're an unexpected but welcome addition.

In a large bowl, combine the pineapple, watermelon, honeydew, mango, and coconut. Drizzle with the lime juice and agave nectar, then sprinkle with the lime zest and mint. Gently toss everything together.

Stud the top of the salad with the raspberries, then drizzle on a bit more lime juice and garnish with a scattering of mint.

ELIZABETH'S TIP

If you can find a fresh coconut and know how crack it open and extract the meat, do it. If not, look for fresh coconut meat in the produce or refrigerated section of well-stocked grocery stores. If you can't find fresh coconut, look for frozen coconut meat and thaw before using.

GLOW HOUR GREEN JUICE PUNCH BOWL

1 cucumber, coarsely chopped

1 green apple, halved, cored, and coarsely chopped

2 limes, peeled and coarsely chopped

2 cups fresh pineapple chunks

1-inch piece fresh ginger, peeled and coarsely chopped

½ small jalapeño chile, seeded

2 cups loosely packed spinach leaves

Small handful of fresh mint leaves

3 cups coconut water

Thin cucumber and lime slices, for serving

SERVES 8

This may be the glow hour, but you can still serve a showstopping NA punch at your party. I love homemade green juice, or let's be real, I also love paying for a twelve-dollar ice-cold fresh juice after a hot yoga class, too. This green juice delivers a good balance of fruity and earthy. Be sure to keep this drink ice-cold when serving, or set a full ice bucket alongside the punch bowl so guests can add cube or two to their glass. If you want to turn the green juice into a cocktail, I recommend adding tequila or vodka.

In a blender, combine the cucumber, apple, limes, pineapple, ginger, jalapeño, spinach, mint, and coconut water and blend until smooth.

Strain the mixture through a fine-mesh strainer twice or through a nut milk bag. Discard the solids. Refrigerate the "juice" in an airtight container until well chilled.

Serve in a punch bowl or pitcher with a bucket of ice and rocks glasses alongside. Garnish with the cucumber and lime slices.

CHINESE CHICKEN SALAD SPRING ROLLS

FOR THE SAUCE

¼ cup tahini

2 tablespoons soy sauce

2 tablespoons rice vinegar

1 tablespoon honey

1 teaspoon Asian sesame oil

1 garlic clove, grated

1-inch piece fresh ginger, peeled and grated

FOR THE ROLLS

12 round rice paper wrappers, each about 9 inches in diameter

½ small savoy cabbage, thinly sliced or shredded

2 large carrots, peeled and shredded

1 bunch green onions, white and green parts, very thinly sliced on the diagonal

2 cups coarsely shredded cooked chicken (about 8 ounces; rotisserie chicken works well)

One 11-ounce can mandarin orange sections in juice or water, drained

1 jalapeño chile, stemmed and very thinly sliced (optional)

1 bunch fresh cilantro, chopped

MAKES 12 ROLLS

One of my all-time favorite places for a light, healthy lunch is Farmhouse at Roger's Gardens in Corona del Mar. I order the Asian chicken salad, which is filled to the brim with fresh vegetables and succulent chicken and is dressed with an umami-rich sesame vinaigrette. Here, that fabulous salad has been repackaged as a tasty handheld spring roll.

TO MAKE THE SAUCE, in a small glass bowl, whisk together the tahini, soy sauce, vinegar, honey, sesame oil, garlic, and ginger until well mixed and smooth. (The sauce can be thinned with 1 or 2 tablespoons of water as needed.) Cover until serving.

TO MAKE THE ROLLS, select a clean work surface, such as a cutting board or a countertop. Prep and then line up all the ingredients you need for the rolls near the work surface: rice paper wrappers, cabbage, carrots, green onions, chicken, mandarin oranges, jalapeño slices (if using), and cilantro. Add warm water to a depth of 1 inch to a large shallow dish and set it near the rice paper rounds. Set a platter nearby for the finished rolls.

Slide a rice paper wrapper into the warm water and leave for 5 seconds or so, just until pliable, then lay the wrapper flat on the work surface and wait for about 1 minute until evenly softened. On the center of the third of the wrapper closest to you, layer a little cabbage, carrot, and green onion, followed by 2 pieces of chicken, 2 mandarin orange segments, a couple of jalapeño slices (if using), and a sprinkle of cilantro. As you work, arrange the ingredients in a long, narrow pile to match the shape of the finished roll. Be careful not to stuff the roll too full. Bring the edge of the roll closest to you up over the filling, covering it, and then fold in both sides and continue rolling up tightly, using your fingers to keep the filling snugly inside the wrapper. Set the roll aside, seam side down, on the platter and repeat with remaining wrappers and filling ingredients.

Serve the rolls right away with the sauce alongside.

ELIZABETH'S TIP

If you are new to working with rice paper wrappers, have a few extra on hand, as they can easily tear or fold over and stick to themselves once they're softened.

Holiday Hideaway

CHEESE YULE LOGS: SPICED AND SAVORY

FOR THE SPICED YULE LOG

4 ounces cream cheese, at room temperature

4 ounces fresh goat cheese, at room temperature

¼ teaspoon ground ginger

¼ teaspoon ground cinnamon

1 tablespoon minced fresh rosemary leaves

Kosher salt and freshly ground black pepper

½ cup finely chopped pecans

½ cup finely chopped dried cranberries

Honey, for drizzling

FOR THE SAVORY YULE LOG

4 ounces cream cheese, at room temperature

1 cup shredded sharp English cheddar cheese

2 tablespoons chopped fresh chives

1 tablespoon minced fresh rosemary leaves

1 teaspoon garlic powder

1 teaspoon onion powder

Kosher salt and freshly ground black pepper

½ cup finely chopped pecans

Crackers or pretzel chips, for serving

MAKES 2 LOGS; EACH LOG SERVES 4

These sweet and savory cheese yule logs are edible holiday decor for your snack table. The spiced log is laced with ginger and cinnamon, with each bite making you feel like you're donning a cozy winter sweater. The savory log is packed with the robust flavors of English cheddar and fresh herbs. Serve the logs side by side.

TO MAKE THE SPICED LOG, in a medium bowl, combine the cream cheese, goat cheese, ginger, cinnamon, rosemary, a hefty pinch of salt, and a few grinds of pepper and mix together until well blended and smooth.

Lay a sheet of plastic wrap on a flat surface and place the cheese mixture in a line down the center. Fold the plastic over the mixture, then press and shape it with your hands into a log about 6 inches long and 1 inch in diameter. Roll the log back and forth to smooth the surface. Wrap tightly and refrigerate for 25 to 30 minutes, or until semi-firm.

Spread the pecans on one end of a sheet pan and the cranberries on the other end. Unwrap the cheese log and roll it first in the pecans and then in the cranberries, coating it evenly each time. Transfer the log to a serving platter and drizzle with honey.

TO MAKE THE SAVORY LOG, in a medium bowl, combine the cream cheese, cheddar, chives, rosemary, garlic powder, onion powder, a hefty pinch of salt, and a few grinds of pepper and mix together until well blended and smooth.

Lay a sheet of plastic wrap on a flat work surface and transfer the cheese mixture to the center of the plastic wrap in a line. Lift the side of the plastic wrap nearest you and fold it over the cheese mixture. Then, using your hands, press and mold the mixture into a rough log about 6 inches long and 2 inches in diameter. Fold in the sides of the plastic wrap and then roll the log back and forth to smooth the surface and create a more uniform shape. Roll up the log in the remaining plastic wrap and refrigerate the wrapped log for 25 to 30 minutes, or until semi-firm.

Spread the pecans on a sheet pan. Unwrap the cheese log and roll in the pecans, coating evenly. Transfer the log to a serving platter.

Serve the logs with crackers.

CRÈME DE CHRISTMAS TREE

1½ ounces half-and-half

1 ounce crème de menthe

1 ounce crème de cacao blanc

½ ounce gin

Sugared rosemary sprig, for garnish

SERVES 1

Oh Christmas tree, Oh Christmas tree, I hope I get a good holiday buzz from thee! And you certainly will. Made with gin plus two liqueurs, this creamy Christmas tree–inspired beverage packs a punch that is guaranteed to get any holiday party off to a great start. If you like, swap out the gin for vodka.

In a cocktail shaker, combine the half-and-half, crème de menthe, crème de cacao blanc, and gin. Add 2 scoops of ice, cover the shaker, and shake hard for 10 to 15 seconds, or until the outside of the shaker is frosty cold to the touch.

Strain into a rocks glass over ice. Garnish with the rosemary sprig.

ELIZABETH'S TIP

This is an easy drink to batch for eight. Add 1½ cups half-and-half, 1 cup each crème de menthe and crème de cacao blanc, and ½ cup gin or vodka to a pitcher and stir to mix. Cover and refrigerate until well chilled. Stir again just before serving, then pour into rocks glasses over ice. Don't forget the sugared rosemary sprigs for garnish!

ISABELLA'S WINTER MULLED CRANBERRY TONIC

2 ounces apple cider or juice

1 ounce unsweetened pure cranberry juice

½ ounce spiced syrup (page 198)

Tonic water, preferably Fever-Tree, for topping

Fresh rosemary sprig and cranberries, for garnish

SERVES 1

ZERO PROOF 0%

My dear friend Isabella is a master barista. She created this sister tonic to the drink below, using the same cranberry juice–based spiced syrup, which can do double duty in both cocktails and mocktails.

Fill a highball or other tall glass with ice. Add the apple juice, cranberry juice, and spiced syrup and stir until well mixed. Top with the tonic water and stir gently. Garnish with the rosemary sprig and cranberries.

ELIZABETH'S TIP

The versatile spiced syrup (page 198) can be used to give any holiday drink a holiday flavor. Swap it in for simple syrup or agave nectar.

SPICED CRANBERRY OLD FASHIONED

2 ounces bourbon or other whiskey

½ ounce unsweetened pure cranberry juice

½ ounce spiced syrup (page 198)

Orange peel, for garnish

SERVES 1

This is the kind of cocktail, with its smoky vanilla bourbon notes and heady spiced syrup, I want late in the evening on Christmas Eve. The presents are wrapped and the only lights on are the Christmas tree twinkles and the TV glow of *Home Alone* playing.

In a mixing glass, combine the bourbon, cranberry juice, and spiced syrup. Fill the glass two-thirds full with ice, then, using a barspoon, stir around the edge of the glass 20 to 30 times, or until well chilled.

Strain into a rocks glass over a large ice cube and garnish with the orange peel.

PIPER-HEIDSIE

SHRIMP COCKTAIL WITH CALABRIAN CHILE SAUCE

Kosher salt

1½ pounds shrimp, peeled and deveined with tail segment intact

FOR THE SAUCE

⅓ cup ketchup

2 tablespoons jarred chopped Calabrian chiles

1 tablespoon prepared horseradish

1 tablespoon fresh lemon juice

2 teaspoons Worcestershire sauce

Lemon wedges, for serving

SERVES 8

This low-fuss appetizer is easy to put together and makes everyone happy. Plump, pink shrimp on a bed of crushed ice are paired with a zippy red cocktail sauce. I lace the sauce with Calabrian chiles, a culinary secret weapon that I use to add fruity, smoky, complex "fire" to tomato-based dishes. Whenever I serve this old-school shrimp platter, I inevitably find someone near it trying to go for "just one more"—I'm looking at you, Marren!

Fill a medium pot three-fourths full with water and add a big pinch of salt. Bring to a boil over high heat. While the water heats, in a large bowl, combine equal parts ice cubes and water.

When the water is boiling, remove the pot from the heat, add the shrimp, and cover the pot. Let the shrimp "cook" in the hot water for 3 to 4 minutes, or until they are opaque and pink.

Using a slotted spoon, transfer the shrimp to the ice bath and let cool for 2 to 3 minutes. Using the slotted spoon, transfer the shrimp to a large plate and blot dry with paper towels.

TO MAKE THE SAUCE, in a small bowl, stir together the ketchup, chiles, horseradish, lemon juice, and Worcestershire sauce, mixing well.

Line a serving platter with crushed ice and arrange the shrimp on top. Serve with the sauce and lemon wedges.

Holiday Games

LET THE MERRIMENT BEGIN!

Some people throw giant Super Bowl parties. Others are experts at hosting birthday celebrations. For me, it has always been Christmas. When I was growing up, my mom put all her energy and creativity into the December holidays, and I know she passed that gene along to me. Each year, I cook up a buffet-style Italian feast (hello, ricotta-stuffed shells, page 184), come up with a fun Christmas craft, put together an epic cocktail spread, and organize some fun holiday games.

Party games are tricky, as they can go from cute to cliché fast. But for some reason, people really push that to the wayside for the holidays. It's a time to get funky and have fun. Bring out the Mrs. Claus costume and rent the snow machine. These are memories that last a lifetime.

CANDY CANE BOBBING

Fill a bucket with stuffing fluff (polyester fiberfill or natural cotton). Place a dozen candy canes in the bucket. Tie another candy cane around the end of a long piece of ribbon or string. Tie a piece of ribbon or string around your waist and attach the candy cane ribbon to the center of the ribbon. The candy cane should swing between your legs (yes, you read that right). Without using your hands, "bob" for the candy canes in the bucket by bending your knees and hooking the canes on your swinging candy cane. Each player has 30 seconds or so, and whoever hooks the most candy canes wins.

BLINDFOLDED BOW GRAB

On your kitchen island, make a messy holiday spread with bowls, ribbons, lottery scratchers, cash, and gift cards. The player is blindfolded and slips a plastic drink cup over each hand (like reindeer antlers) or grasps a plastic spatula in each hand. They have 30 to 60 seconds to pick up whatever they can and put it into a bowl. Whatever makes it into the bowl, the player gets to keep.

COZY CROSSWORD
Fast $20 Spot
your letters
PRIZE KEY
CALL
SHRUB
OUTYOURSELF
PROGRAM
NINETEEN
WIN UP TO $20,000!
COZY CROSSWORD
COZY CROSSWORD
JEWEL
EXAMPLE
SURGE

RICOTTA-PESTO STUFFED SHELLS WITH MARINARA

FOR THE FILLING

One 15-ounce container whole-milk ricotta cheese

¼ cup homemade or store-bought pesto (I like Rana brand)

2 packed cups spinach leaves, finely chopped

½ cup grated Parmigiano-Reggiano cheese

1 egg, whisked

1 teaspoon garlic powder

1 teaspoon Italian seasoning

Kosher salt

One 12-ounce box jumbo pasta shells

3 cups store-bought marinara sauce

2 cups shredded mozzarella cheese

¼ cup homemade or store-bought pesto

Chopped fresh flat-leaf parsley, for garnish

SERVES 8

When these Italian-inspired stuffed pasta shells are baking in the oven, the smell transports me back to our family kitchen with my mom wearing a Christmas sweater and holiday songs playing. She always made this cozy dish of ricotta-packed shells as appetizers for our yuletide parties. Sometimes I cook a pound of bulk Italian sausage and add it to the filling if I feel like I want meaty flavor, but the choice is yours.

TO MAKE THE FILLING, in a medium bowl, combine the ricotta, pesto, spinach, cheese, egg, garlic powder, Italian seasoning, and a pinch of salt and stir together until smooth and creamy. Transfer the filling to a large resealable bag, secure the bag closed, and refrigerate until using.

Fill a large pot three-fourths full with generously salted water and bring to a boil over high heat. Add the pasta shells, stir well, and cook for 7 to 8 minutes, or according to the package directions for al dente.

While the pasta is cooking, pour 2¼ cups of the marinara sauce on the bottom of an 8-by-10-inch baking dish. Set aside. Preheat the oven to 350°F.

When the pasta shells are ready, drain into a colander and rinse under cool running water until cool enough to touch. Drain well.

Snip off a lower corner of the resealable bag with the filling. Holding a shell in your nondominant hand, pipe the filling into the shell, then set the shell, filling side up, in the prepared baking dish. Fill the remaining shells the same way, adding them to the dish. They should fit snugly.

Scatter the mozzarella evenly over the filled shells, then drizzle with the pesto and the remaining ¾ cup marinara. Bake for 30 to 35 minutes, or until the sauce is bubbling and the top is golden.

Remove from the oven, top with the parsley, and serve.

ELIZABETH'S TIP

These shells take a bit of prep time to cook, fill, and assemble. I always make them the morning of the party and pop them into the oven to finish about a half hour before people arrive.

SANTA'S SPRITZ

1 ounce gin

1 ounce pomegranate juice

1 ounce fresh orange juice

½ ounce Campari

2 to 3 ounces prosecco

Pomegranate seeds, fresh or sugared rosemary sprig, and/or dehydrated orange wheel, for garnish

SERVES 1

If there is anyone who deserves a holiday happy hour, it's Santa. This drink is as deep red as Santa's suit and is perfectly jolly. Serve this spritz as the first drink of the night to get everyone into the holiday spirit. Its fruity flavors of pomegranate and orange alongside bold Campari and gin make it extra festive.

Fill a large cocktail glass or wineglass with ice. Add the gin, pomegranate juice, orange juice, and Campari and stir gently. Top with the prosecco and again stir gently. Garnish with the pomegranate seeds, rosemary sprig, and/or dehydrated orange wheel.

FIREPLACE HOT TODDY

6 cups apple cider

2 cups bourbon or other whiskey

1 orange, thinly sliced

3 cinnamon sticks, plus more for garnish

2-inch piece fresh ginger, peeled and thinly sliced lengthwise

2 fresh rosemary sprigs, plus more for garnish

Orange or apple slices, for garnish

SERVES 8 TO 10

When I was twenty, I left home for the whole month of December and spent my first Christmas away from my family. It was a soft and reflective time that had me searching for small moments of comfort. Anytime I drink a boozy, warm beverage, I feel like I am once again walking around Christmas markets in London during that growing season of my life. This hot toddy is warming, cozy, and exactly what you want to offer to someone who just came in from the cold.

In a Dutch oven over medium-high heat, combine the apple cider, bourbon, orange slices, cinnamon sticks, ginger, and rosemary and bring to a simmer. Turn down the heat to low and simmer gently for 30 to 60 minutes to deepen the flavors. Scoop out the ginger slices and discard.

To serve, ladle into a mug and garnish with the cinnamon sticks, rosemary sprigs, and orange slices.

ELIZABETH'S TIP

This is a great recipe for a party, as it yields a big batch. You can easily make a NA version by simply skipping the bourbon or by adding a nonalcoholic substitute, such as Ritual Zero Proof Whiskey Alternative.

SCRABBLE

Menu

Holiday spirits served here! A holiday cocktail menu should be both a little whimsical and have a wintry feel. Start with festive vodka martinis and spicy shrimp cocktail. The morning of the party, whip up a batch of ricotta-stuffed shells and slide them into the oven a half hour before party time.

Happy Holidays!

CRANBERRY ORANGE PASTRY

FOR THE CREAM CHEESE FILLING

4 ounces cream cheese, at room temperature

Grated zest of ½ orange

½ cup powdered sugar

FOR THE CRANBERRY FILLING

1 cup fresh cranberries

2 tablespoons dark brown sugar

½ teaspoon ground cinnamon

Grated zest of ½ orange

¼ cup fresh orange juice

2 sheets puff pastry (about 9 ounce each), thawed according to package directions

1 egg, whisked, for egg wash

Turbinado sugar, for sprinkling

Powdered sugar, for dusting (optional)

MAKES 12 PASTRIES

When you think of happy hour, I'm sure you think of such classics as chips and dip, a cheese board, chicken wings, sliders, and the like. This is me giving you permission to offer a little something sweet alongside the savory. Plus, since this is the holiday chapter, there are no rules, so the greater the variety of treats, the better! These little puff pastries conceal two of the best flavors of winter—cranberry and orange—and look elegant on any spread. Pair them with a glass of Champagne or a Spiced Clove Mimosa (page 194).

TO MAKE THE CHEESE FILLING, in a small bowl, combine the cream cheese, orange zest, and powdered sugar and mix until smooth. Cover and refrigerate until using.

TO MAKE THE CRANBERRY FILLING, in a small saucepan, stir together the cranberries, brown sugar, cinnamon, and orange zest and juice. Place over medium heat and bring to a simmer, stirring often. Turn down the heat to low and cook, stirring occasionally, for about 8 minutes, or until the cranberries begin to pop and the mixture resembles a thick smashed jam. You want some cranberries to remain intact. Remove from heat and let cool completely.

Preheat the oven to 400°F. Line a large sheet pan with parchment paper.

Cut each pastry sheet into six rectangles. Arrange the pastries slightly apart on the prepared sheet pan.

Scoop some cream cheese filling onto the center of each pastry and spread it in an even layer, leaving a ½-inch border on all sides. Dollop the cooled cranberry mixture evenly on top of each cream cheese layer. Using a paring knife or fork, lightly score the border of each pastry. Using a pastry brush, brush the border of each pastry with the egg wash. Lightly sprinkle the pastry borders with turbinado sugar.

Bake the pastries for 18 to 20 minutes, or until puffed and golden brown. Let cool on the pan on a wire rack for 10 to 15 minutes, then sift powdered sugar on top of each pastry, if desired.

Cut into rectangles or squares, transfer to a board or platter, and serve.

SPICED CLOVE MIMOSA

1 ounce spiced clove syrup (page 199)

2 ounces orange juice

3 to 4 ounces Champagne or prosecco

SERVES 1

Christmas morning may just be the happiest of hours at the holiday hideaway. Such celebrations call for bottomless mimosas with a spiced holiday essence. This warming clove syrup can be used with sparkling apple cider for a quick zero-proof version of the drink. I highly recommend double batching if you're serving these for a gathering. They go quickly!

In a champagne flute or coupe, combine the clove syrup and orange juice and stir to mix. Top with the Champagne and stir once.

EXQUIS!
MAISON FONDÉE
EN 1883
MOËT

SUGAR PLUM MARTINI

Sugar and lemon wedge, for rimming the glass

2 ounces vodka

1 ounce fresh lemon juice

½ ounce white cranberry juice

1 teaspoon plum jam (see Elizabeth's Tip)

Pear slice and sugared or fresh cranberries, for garnish (optional)

SERVES 1

Every year, my friends get a paper invitation in the mail for a Christmas party at the Sugar Plum Chalet—aka my house. It's a cute touch that makes the night and the theme feel a bit more magical. This dressed-up vodka martini is bright, wintry, and whimsical—not to mention on theme. Each martini is shaken with a little sweet plum jam to make sure *The Nutcracker* theme is in every guest's glass.

Place a thin layer of sugar onto a flat saucer. Rub the outside rim of a martini glass with the lemon wedge, then holding the glass at an angle almost parallel to the saucer, roll the dampened edge in the sugar to coat. Set the glass aside.

In a cocktail shaker, combine the vodka, lemon juice, cranberry juice, and jam. Add 2 scoops of ice, cover the shaker, and shake hard for 10 to 15 seconds, or until the outside of the shaker is frosty cold to the touch.

Strain into the sugar-rimmed martini glass. Garnish with a pear slice and fresh cranberries, if desired.

ELIZABETH'S TIP

If you can't find plum jam, you can swap in apricot or peach jam for a pretty pink hue.

SUGAR OR SPICE: SYRUPS FOR ANY DRINK

Here are eight syrups for adding a sweet note to a classic cocktail or a splash of flavor to tonic or soda water for a no-fuss mocktail. They'll keep in an airtight container in the refrigerator for up to 2 weeks.

SIMPLE SYRUP

½ cup sugar
½ cup water

In a small saucepan over medium heat, combine the sugar and water and bring to a simmer, stirring constantly until the sugar fully dissolves. Let cool.

Makes 1½ cups

SPICED SYRUP

½ cup unsweetened cranberry juice
½ cup packed light brown sugar
½ cup maple syrup
4 cinnamon sticks, broken in half
10 whole star anise
2 teaspoons whole cloves
1 teaspoon ground allspice

In a small saucepan over medium heat, combine all the ingredients and bring to a simmer, stirring. Turn down the heat to low and simmer, stirring, for about 5 minutes, or until the sugar has dissolved. Remove from the heat and let steep for about 30 minutes, then strain through a fine-mesh strainer and let cool.

Makes 1 cup

HIBISCUS SYRUP

1 cup water
1 cup sugar
1 cup dried hibiscus flowers

In a small saucepan over medium heat, combine the sugar and water and bring to a simmer, stirring constantly until the sugar fully dissolves. Remove from the heat, add the flowers, stir briefly, and let steep for 10 to 15 minutes, then pour through a fine-mesh strainer and let cool.

Makes 1½ cups

BASIL SYRUP

½ cup sugar
½ cup water
1 cup fresh basil leaves

In a small saucepan over medium heat, combine the sugar and water and bring to a simmer, stirring constantly until the sugar fully dissolves. Remove from the heat, add the basil, stir briefly, and let steep for 20 to 30 minutes, then pour through a fine-mesh strainer and let cool.

Makes ¾ cup

HONEY SYRUP

⅓ cup honey
⅓ cup water

In a small microwave-safe bowl, combine the honey and water and microwave in bursts of 5 to 8 seconds, stirring after each burst, just until the honey thins and dissolves. Alternatively, warm in a small saucepan over low heat on the stovetop just until the honey dissolves. Let cool.

Makes ⅔ cup

COCONUT SYRUP

1 cup water
1 cup sugar
½ cup unsweetened dried coconut flakes

In a small saucepan over medium heat, combine the sugar and water and bring to a simmer, stirring constantly until the sugar fully dissolves. Remove from the heat, add the coconut, stir briefly, and let steep for 15 to 25 minutes (timing depends on desired flavor strength), then pour through a fine-mesh strainer and let cool.

Makes 1½ cups

HONEY TURMERIC SYRUP

½ cup water
½ cup honey
1 teaspoon ground turmeric
1 teaspoon ground ginger
Pinch of black pepper

In a small saucepan over medium-low heat, combine all the ingredients and bring to a gentle simmer, stirring often. Simmer gently, stirring occasionally, for 5 to 10 minutes, or until fragrant. Remove from the heat, pour through a fine-mesh strainer, and let cool.

Makes 1 cup

SPICED CLOVE SYRUP

1 cup sugar
1 cup water
Peel from 1 orange
2 tablespoons whole cloves
2 cinnamon sticks, broken in half

In a small saucepan over medium heat, combine all the ingredients and bring to a simmer, stirring constantly, until the sugar fully dissolves. Turn down the heat to low and simmer gently, stirring occasionally, for 15 minutes, or until fragrant. Let cool, then pour through a fine-mesh strainer.

Makes 1½ cups

Coast to Coast

PEACH WHITE LINEN

5 cucumber slices

3 peach slices

1½ ounces gin

½ ounce peach liqueur

1 ounce fresh lemon juice

Honey to taste

1 to 2 ounces club soda

Peach slice and cucumber slices, for garnish

SERVES 1

This is exactly what you want to be sipping while nestled in a cozy coastal spot with a grandma hobby in hand. A fruity riff on the classic white linen, this refreshing drink is made with smashed summer peaches and cucumbers, gin, and subtly sweet peach liqueur. Pair it with a jigsaw puzzle, a round of mah-jongg, a fresh needlepoint canvas (my personal favorite), or a new paint-by-number watercolor painting.

Put the cucumber and peach slices into a cocktail shaker and muddle until they are slightly smashed and have released their juices. Add the gin, peach liqueur, lemon juice, and honey and stir together with a barspoon until the honey has thinned and is fully dissolved.

Add 2 scoops of ice to the shaker, cover the shaker, and shake hard for 10 to 15 seconds, or until the outside of the shaker is frosty cold to the touch.

Strain into a rocks glass over ice. Top with the club soda and stir gently. Garnish with the peach slice and cucumber slices.

COASTLINE MINI CRAB CAKES WITH RÉMOULADE

FOR THE CRAB CAKES

½ cup mayonnaise

1 egg, whisked

1 tablespoon Dijon mustard

½ teaspoon Old Bay Seasoning

1 tablespoon Worcestershire sauce

1 pound jumbo lump crabmeat, picked over for shell fragments

¾ cup panko bread crumbs

¼ cup olive oil, for frying

Kosher salt

FOR THE RÉMOULADE

½ cup mayonnaise

1 tablespoon Dijon mustard

1 tablespoon finely chopped fresh chives

1 garlic clove, grated

1 teaspoon Worcestershire sauce

1 teaspoon fresh lemon juice

½ teaspoon Old Bay Seasoning

¼ teaspoon smoked paprika

⅛ teaspoon cayenne pepper

Chopped fresh chives, for garnish

Lemon wedges, for serving

MAKES 8 TO 12 CRAB CAKES

Crab cakes are one of those dishes for which nearly everyone has a favorite cake they've coined or a sacred family recipe they use. While I cannot guarantee these have a heritage background, I can guarantee they are scrumptious and very easy to make. I serve them alongside a perfectly spiced rémoulade that's so good you can literally drink it. (It's very tasty with fries too!)

TO MAKE THE CRAB CAKES, in a medium bowl, combine the mayonnaise, egg, mustard, Old Bay Seasoning, and Worcestershire sauce and stir until smooth. Add the crabmeat and panko and gently fold together just until combined. Cover and refrigerate for at least 1 hour or up to 4 hours.

TO MAKE THE RÉMOULADE, in a small bowl, whisk together the mayonnaise, mustard, chives, garlic, Worcestershire sauce, lemon juice, Old Bay Seasoning, paprika, and cayenne until smooth. Cover and refrigerate until serving.

To shape each cake, scoop up about 3 tablespoons of the chilled crab mixture and shape into a round ½ inch to 1 inch thick, setting the cakes aside on a plate as they are shaped.

Line a large plate with paper towels and set it near the stove. In a large skillet, heat the oil over medium heat until it shimmers. Add about half of the crab cakes, being careful not to crowd the pan, and cook, turning once, for about 3 minutes on each side, or until golden brown on both sides. As the cakes are ready, transfer to the towel-lined plate to drain and sprinkle lightly with salt. Repeat with the remaining cakes.

Transfer the crab cakes to a serving platter or napkin-lined basket. Top with the chives and serve hot with the rémoulade and lemon wedges.

ELIZABETH'S TIP

While I know this is a happy hour book, I feel obligated to tell you that these make a fantastic main course for dinner, too. Simply make 4 to 6 large cakes rather than 8 to 12 small ones.

OYSTERS WITH PONZU MIGNONETTE

FOR THE PONZU MIGNONETTE

¼ cup ponzu sauce (see Elizabeth's Tip)

1 tablespoon water

1 teaspoon Asian sesame oil

1½ green onions, white and green parts, very finely diced

1½ teaspoons grated, peeled fresh ginger

¼ teaspoon sesame seeds

Grated zest of ½ lime

12 to 24 oysters, freshly shucked

Crushed ice, for serving

SERVES 4

Some people may come after me, but I am going to say it anyway: I don't particularly like mignonette. There, I said it. I'm just not a big vinegar girl! But I *love* this ponzu riff on the classic condiment. A bright, citrusy, gingery soy sauce mix, it delivers the same punchy flavor as the traditional mignonette and nicely levels up these oysters or nearly any other raw seafood. A platter of these oysters and an ice-cold bottle of Champagne are the ideal sunset snack at your favorite beachside perch. If you'd like, ask a seafood counter attendant to shuck your oysters for you. No one will know except you and the seafood clerk, and there is something romantic about that (ha!).

TO MAKE THE MIGNONETTE, in a small bowl, whisk together the ponzu sauce, water, sesame oil, green onions, ginger, sesame seeds, and lime zest, mixing well. Cover and refrigerate for at least 30 minutes to allow the flavors to develop. You can serve the mignonette right away, but letting it sit for even a short time ensures optimum flavor. The mignonette can be refrigerated for up to 2 days. Give it a quick stir before serving.

TO SHUCK THE OYSTERS, scrub the oysters clean. Line a platter with crushed ice. Holding an oyster cup side down in a towel (or glove), insert a knife into the hinge and pry open. Slide the knife under the top shell to sever the muscle and discard the shell. Remove any grit, loosen the oyster from the bottom shell without spilling the liquor, and nestle it into the ice. Repeat.

Line a large serving platter with crushed ice. Nestle the oysters in the half shell in the ice. Set the bowl of mignonette with a small spoon on or alongside the platter of oysters and serve.

ELIZABETH'S TIP

Ponzu sauce is made from citrus juice, soy sauce, mirin, sugar, and, yes, vinegar. Look for it in bottles in Japanese markets and well-stocked supermarkets.

THE SUN-TEA-NI

FOR THE SUN TEA CONCENTRATE
10 tea bags, preferably black tea

5 cups water

FOR THE HONEY SYRUP
2 teaspoons honey

2 teaspoons water

FOR THE COCKTAIL
1½ ounces gin

½ ounce Cointreau or other orange liqueur

½ ounce fresh lemon juice

2 teaspoons honey syrup

1 ounce sun tea concentrate

Thin lemon slice and fresh mint leaves, for garnish

SERVES 1

FOR THE SUN-TEA-NI BATCH COCKTAILS
In a medium pitcher, combine 1½ cups gin, ½ cup Cointreau or other orange liqueur, ½ cup fresh lemon juice, ⅔ cup honey syrup (page 199), and 1 cup sun tea concentrate and stir to mix well. Cover and refrigerate until well chilled. Stir again just before serving, then serve in chilled martini glasses and garnish with lemon slices and mint leaves.

SERVES 8

The Sun-Tea-Ni is the Arnold Palmer martini—a golfer's best wingman. When I was growing up in sunny California, my dad always had a jug of sun tea brewing on the porch. That memory inspired this cocktail. For flavor, you can add lemons, oranges, peaches, or other fruits with the tea bags and then scoop them out with the bags. This recipe yields a large amount of tea concentrate. You can also dilute it with water for iced tea, or you can make a batch of this homage to the Arnold Palmer for sipping with friends on a long summer afternoon.

TO MAKE THE SUN TEA CONCENTRATE, combine the tea bags and water in a 2-quart clear glass container or drink dispenser and seal closed. Set the container outdoors in direct sunlight and let the tea steep for 2 hours. Remove and discard the tea bags and then refrigerate until using. The tea will keep up to 1 week.

TO MAKE THE HONEY SYRUP, in a small microwave-safe bowl, combine the honey and water and microwave for 5 to 8 seconds, or until the honey thins and dissolves. Remove from the microwave, stir well, and let sit just until cool. Alternatively, combine the honey and water in a small saucepan and heat over low heat on the stovetop until the honey dissolves.

TO MAKE THE COCKTAIL, in a cocktail shaker, combine the gin, Cointreau, lemon juice, honey syrup, and sun tea concentrate. Add 2 scoops of ice, cover the shaker, and shake hard for 10 to 15 seconds, or until the outside of the shaker is frosty cold to the touch.

Strain into a chilled martini glass and garnish with the lemon slice and mint leaf.

ELIZABETH'S TIP

Don't be tempted to add honey rather than honey syrup to the cocktail shaker, as honey will stick to the ice, leaving you with a flavorless, unsweetened drink.

El Velero
WHITE TUNA
IN OLIVE OIL

TIN FISH SNACK SPREAD

5 to 7 cans assorted preserved fish

1 block hard cheese, such as Gruyère or Cheddar

1 wheel Brie cheese

1 bunch radishes, trimmed and halved lengthwise

1 lemon, cut into wedges

½ cup cornichons, halved

4 to 5 hard-boiled eggs, peeled and halved

½ cup roasted Marcona almonds

½ cup pitted green olives, such as Castelvetrano or Picholine

3 tablespoons whole-grain mustard

Butter, for serving

½ sleeve saltine crackers

2 cups kettle potato chips

6 to 8 baguette slices, toasted

SERVES 8 TO 10

Meet the Tin Fish Snack Spread—or what I like to call "the lazy girl cheese board"—that delivers all the variety and little bites you get in a good cheese or charcuterie board with less fussing by the host. The petite cans of fish do most of the work for you. Grab a good mix of tins, such as octopus, sardines, smoked salmon, tuna, and mackerel, and pair them with toasted bread, salty crackers, olives, and mustard. To make it more of a party board, add items like slices of hard cheese, wedges of Brie or Camembert, roasted nuts, store-bought pickled vegetables, and some creamy French butter.

Line a large sheet pan with parchment paper.

Open each can of tinned fish and place it on the prepared sheet pan. Slice the hard cheese into triangles and cut the Brie into wedges and arrange around the tins of fish on the sheet pan. Fill in any spaces with the radishes, lemon wedges, cornichons, hard-boiled eggs, almonds, olives, mustard (in a small dish), butter (in a crock or small dish), crackers, potato chips, and toasted bread.

Serve with small forks, spoons, and spreaders.

ELIZABETH'S TIP

I love gathering cans of fish and two or three other items from this board for a quick host gift or housewarming present. Wrap up everything in a cute reusable basket and add a bottle of Champagne.

ORTIZ
El Velero
WHITE TUNA
IN OLIVE OIL
AND TOMATO SAUCE
MABOTI
PRODUCED AND PACKED BY
PINHAIS & C.ª L.DA
MATOSINHOS-PORTUGAL
NET WT. 3.17 OZ(90g)
MATOSINHOS - PORTUGAL
"Nuri"
NET WEIGHT 4.4 OZ (125g)
Octopus
in Extra Virgin Olive Oil
MORGADA
PORTUGAL
NET WT. / PESO LÍQ.
3.9 oz / 110 g
Los aventuras de una Sardina en las Brasas
GÜEYUMAR
CONSERVAS BRASEADAS
ORTIZ
El Velero
NET WT
3.95oz
(112g)
WHITE TUNA
IN OLIVE OIL
LITTLE SPAIN
Chipirones en su tinta
SQUIDS IN INK
PRODUCT OF SPAIN
NET WT 3.91oz (111g)
DR WT 2.46oz (70g)
SQUIDS IN INK
SMOKED SALMON
100% Traceable
Fishwife
Tinned Seafood Co
Responsibly Raised in Norway
WILD. ALL NATURAL. HAND PACKED — HIGH IN PROTEIN
MACKEREL
SIESTA CO
IN OLIVE OIL
ORGANIC OLIVE OIL • NET WT. 4 3/8 oz (124G)
LOS ANGELES, CA — A PIECE OF SPAIN

GIN MARTINI AND TONIC

1½ ounces gin

½ ounce vermouth

½ ounce olive brine

2 to 3 ounces tonic water

Fresh rosemary sprig, green olive, and lemon wedge, for garnish

SERVES 1

Elegant, minimalist, crystalline, and urbane, the gin martini is the ultimate beverage of class—a cocktail to be sipped at a sleek cocktail lounge or a lively piano bar. We jokingly deemed this sophisticated sipper for Nicole Kidman's character, Celeste, in *Big Little Lies*, who was often seen standing outside her chic California abode pondering life with a glass in hand. And it would be equally at home with Nicole on Nantucket with her character in *The Perfect Couple*. This is the kind of drink to enjoy while wrapped in a blanket on a cold coastal night. The tonic water surprisingly and pleasantly plays with the briny notes in a dirty martini.

In a mixing glass, combine the gin, vermouth, and olive brine. Fill the glass two-thirds full with ice, then, using a barspoon, stir around the edge of the glass 20 to 30 times, or until well chilled.

Strain into a wineglass or highball over ice. Top with the tonic water and stir gently. Garnish with the rosemary sprig, olive, and lemon wedge.

ELIZABETH'S TIP

For a liquor-forward drink like this, I recommend using a good-quality gin, like the French-made Citadelle Jardin d'Été or Hendrick's from Scotland, and a first-rate tonic water, such as Fever-Tree.

APE
OD
le Cooked
o Chips

CAPE COD CHARCUTERIE CHIPS

One 8-ounce bag Cape Cod Original potato chips

½ cup arugula

8 thin prosciutto slices, each slice torn into 6 or 8 strips

2 tablespoons plus 2 teaspoons fig jam

Honey, for drizzling

Shredded Parmigiano-Reggiano cheese, for sprinkling

SERVES 4

If you've spent any time on any coast in the summer, chances are you've snacked on a bag of Cape Cod chips. To make this simple appetizer or on-the-go snack, grab a package of the legendary kettle-cooked chips and a few charcuterie items, cut the bag open, and layer the toppings right inside the chip bag. Pair this super-easy charcuterie board in a bag with a chilled bottle of your favorite rosé or pink prosecco or, for a celebration, a top-notch Champagne.

Lay the unopened chips bag flat on a work surface. Using scissors, carefully cut the bag open lengthwise down the center. Then cut open the sides of the bag until the chips are fully exposed, cutting off some of the bag if needed.

Layer the arugula evenly over the chips and then top with the prosciutto strips and dollops of the fig jam. Finish with a light drizzle of honey and a generous scattering of Parmigiano-Reggiano.

Salt

PAPPA'S WHIPPED BUTTER TOWER WITH PRETZELS

½ cup (1 stick) unsalted butter, at room temperature

2 tablespoons milk or water

Flaky sea salt

Large sourdough hard pretzels, for serving (I like Snyder's of Hanover brand)

SERVES 4

If there is one man who knows how to nosh, it's my pappa. The man has introduced me to the simplicity of butter. Every summer we head to Pennsylvania to our family cabin, and our snack game is *strong*. Pappa is famous for breaking out the butter and pretzels. At first I thought he was crazy, but then I tried it. The salty crunch of the pretzel with the creaminess of the butter really is an elite, quick-to-assemble snack. This whipped version takes it one step further.

In a stand mixer fitted with the paddle attachment or in a medium bowl with a handheld mixer, combine the butter and milk and beat on low speed for 1 to 2 minutes, or until well blended. Increase the speed to high and beat for 2 to 4 minutes, or until very light and creamy (see Elizabeth's Tip). Transfer to a serving dish.

Top the whipped butter with a sprinkle of salt and serve with the pretzels.

ELIZABETH'S TIP

For extra flavor, stir roasted garlic, chopped fresh herbs, honey or honeycomb pieces, or grated orange, lemon, or lime zest to taste into the whipped butter.

JOKER
Joker
JOKER

BOOZY PEACHES AND CREAM

FOR THE PEACHES
One 750 ml bottle rosé

¾ cup sugar

Peel of 1 lemon, in strips

3 tablespoons fresh lemon juice

1 vanilla bean

4 peaches, halved and pitted

Vanilla ice cream, for serving

Chopped pistachios, for garnish

SERVES 4 TO 8

When it comes to peak-summer coastal fruits, I am a fiend for peaches. And when the peaches are slowly poached in a whole bottle of rosé (yes, you can use an inexpensive bottle) along with lemon, vanilla, and sugar and served with ice cream (or whipped cream if preferred), you know you will be sitting down to a snack or dessert you won't soon forget. Peaches and cream is a classic pairing for good reason!

TO PREPARE THE PEACHES, in a large skillet or sauté pan, combine the rosé, sugar, lemon peel, and lemon juice. Using a sharp paring knife, split the vanilla bean in half lengthwise, then, using the tip of the knife, scrape out the vanilla seeds into a small bowl. If serving the peaches with whipped cream, measure out ½ teaspoon vanilla seeds and reserve for making the whipped cream. Add the remaining vanilla seeds and the pod halves to the pan with the wine and stir everything together. Add the peaches, skin sides up, to the pan in a single layer.

Place the pan over medium-high heat and bring the mixture to a simmer. Then turn the peaches over, turn down the heat to medium-low, and continue to cook for 10 to 15 minutes, or until a fork inserted into the center of a peach meets only slight resistance. Using a slotted spoon, transfer the peach halves to a medium bowl.

Heat the poaching liquid over medium-high heat, stirring frequently, for about 20 minutes, or until it thickens to a thin syrup. Remove from the heat, strain through a fine-mesh strainer into a small heatproof bowl and let cool. Discard the solids. The syrup will thicken a bit as it cools.

Let the peaches cool completely, then cover and refrigerate until chilled before serving (see Elizabeth's Tip).

To serve, place 1 or 2 peach halves on each individual serving plate and add 1 to 2 scoops of ice cream alongside. Drizzle the peaches with the rosé syrup and finish with a shower of pistachios.

ELIZABETH'S TIP

The peaches are also good served warm. Once you have removed them from the poaching liquid, cover the bowl to keep them warm while you make the rosé syrup (nest the syrup bowl in an ice bath to cool it down quickly). Then serve the peaches warm, drizzled with the syrup, and accompanied with the ice cream.

RASPBERRY SHRUB

FOR THE SHRUB SYRUP

1 cup water

1 cup sugar

1½ cups raspberries, lightly smashed

1 cup apple cider vinegar

FOR THE SHRUB

1 to 2 ounces shrub syrup

Club soda, for topping

Raspberries and fresh rosemary sprig, for garnish

SERVES 1

Buckle up for a brief beverage-history lesson. The "shrub" is such an interesting concept. Back in the day (like the eighteenth century), shrubs were two things: Liqueurs made with vinegar, sugar, and whatever fresh fruit folks were trying to preserve from that season's harvest, and palate-challenging cocktails made with a vinegared syrup, the local hard liquor, and bubbly or non-bubbly water. Nowadays, they're most commonly syrups known as drinking vinegars and are used as tangy flavor boosters in cocktails and mocktails. An homage to the centuries-old shrub, this raspberry vinegar–based drink is bubbly and refreshing but also supports digestion (who doesn't love that?!) and blood sugar control.

TO MAKE THE SHRUB SYRUP, in a small saucepan over medium heat, whisk together the water and sugar for 4 to 5 minutes, or until the sugar is fully dissolved and the mixture is clear. Add the raspberries and vinegar and simmer, stirring occasionally, for about 5 minutes, or until the syrup is a deep raspberry color. Remove from the heat and let cool, then transfer to a glass jar, cap tightly, and store in the refrigerator for up to 6 months. You will have enough syrup to make about 8 drinks.

TO MAKE THE SHRUB, add a scoop of ice to a tall glass. Add the shrub syrup, then top with the club soda and stir gently. Garnish with the raspberries and a rosemary sprig.

HAPPY HOUR
Since 1829
Yuengling
Premium Beer
AMERICA'S OLDEST BREWERS

Half Off at the Dive Bar

CHIPOTLE BARBECUE WINGS

FOR THE WINGS

2 teaspoons light brown sugar

1 teaspoon chipotle chile powder

1 teaspoon smoked paprika

1 teaspoon garlic powder

½ teaspoon kosher salt

Freshly ground black pepper

2 pounds chicken wings

Olive oil cooking spray, for the wings

FOR THE SAUCE

½ cup store-bought barbecue sauce

1 tablespoon unsalted butter, melted

Juice of ½ lime

¼ teaspoon chipotle chile powder

Carrot and celery sticks, for serving

SERVES 4 TO 6

My brother's food pyramid consists of barbecue sauce at the base and all other food groups wedged in somewhere above. He is a connoisseur of all things barbecue, and I know he endorses these finger-licking, spicy, crisp chipotle-kissed chicken wings. They have a deep smoky-sweet flavor that's seriously addictive. Pair them with a crisp, cold IPA and a Sunday night football game.

Preheat the oven to 400°F. Line a large sheet pan with parchment paper or aluminum foil and top with one large or two smaller oven-safe wire racks.

TO PREPARE THE WINGS, first, make the dry rub. In a small bowl, stir together the sugar, chile powder, paprika, garlic powder, salt, and a few grinds of pepper, mixing well.

Pat the chicken wings dry with paper towels, then sprinkle the dry rub evenly on both sides of the wings. Place the wings on the rack on the sheet pan, spacing them evenly apart.

Spray the wings lightly with olive oil spray. Bake the wings, flipping them over halfway through cooking, for about 30 minutes, or until crispy and golden and an instant-read thermometer inserted into the thickest part of a wing not touching bone registers 165°F.

TO MAKE THE SAUCE, while the wings are baking, in a small bowl, whisk together the barbecue sauce, butter, lime juice, and chipotle seasoning, mixing well.

When the wings are ready, remove the pan from the oven and turn on the broiler. Brush the top of each wing with a light layer of the sauce. Place the pan under the broiler and broil the wings for 2 to 3 minutes, or until golden and crispy. Remove the pan from the broiler, flip the wings, and brush the second side with a light layer of the sauce. Return the pan to the broiler and broil for 2 to 3 minutes, or until golden and crispy.

Remove the pan from the broiler and transfer the wings to a serving platter. Toss or brush with the remaining sauce and serve.

BAVARIA

MERMAID JUICE

12 ounces vodka

1½ ounces blue curaçao

10 ounces lemonade

6 ounces pineapple juice

4 ounces fresh lime juice

Swedish Fish candies, shark gummy candies, and pineapple starfish, for serving

SERVES 4

Drinks like Fat Tuesday's frozen Jungle Juice and various tiki bars' fishbowls are in a league of their own. And if I'm being honest, they're a little too artificial and a little too sweet for me. But not this redesigned fishbowl! Unlike the fishbowls of our college years, this one is filled with fresh juices, vodka, and just a splash of blue curaçao for the signature blue hue. I considered calling it the shark tank, so that should tell you exactly just how truly whimsical this party drink is meant to be!

In a large glass fishbowl, combine the vodka, blue curaçao, lemonade, pineapple juice, and lime juice and stir together until well mixed.

Fill the fishbowl with ice. I love to use crunchy pebble ice for this communal drink. Stud the fishbowl with Swedish Fish, shark gummy candies, and starfish cut from pineapple slices. Serve with four long straws and mini umbrellas.

BLOODY MEREDITH

3 cups good-quality tomato juice, chilled

Juice of 1 lemon

2 tablespoons sriracha sauce

2 teaspoons Old Bay Seasoning

2 teaspoons prepared horseradish

1½ to 2 teaspoons celery salt

1 teaspoon soy sauce

1 teaspoon freshly ground black pepper

Celery sticks, lemon wedges, green olives, crisp bacon, and/or cornichons, for a simple garnish

Shrimp skewer, cheese cubes, sliders, mini pretzel bites, and/or mini corn dogs, for a fancy garnish

SERVES 4

ZERO PROOF 0% ZERO PROOF

The best drinks are the ones that come with a snack. That way, they're more than just a drink. They're a small meal—and, in this case, a good hangover cure as well. If you have fun toppings set up from which friends can pick and choose, I recommend making a double batch of the Bloody Meredith mix, as everyone will want seconds. The homemade mix includes seven different seasonings and spices because "being young and beautiful is not a crime, ya know," according to Meredith Blake.

In a small pitcher, combine the tomato juice, lemon juice, sriracha, Old Bay Seasoning, horseradish, celery salt (use 2 teaspoons if you favor a saltier sip), soy sauce, and pepper. Whisk together until all the ingredients are well blended and the mixture is smooth.

Fill four highball glasses or other tall glasses with ice. Pour in the tomato mixture, dividing it evenly. Garnish with your toppers of choice or let your guests dress up their own drink.

ELIZABETH'S TIP

To turn these drinks into a Bloody Mary, add 1½ to 2 ounces vodka or gin to each glass before pouring in the tomato mixture, then stir together.

Menu

Everyone has a local neighborhood dive bar engrained in their memory. Nights filled with karaoke, rounds of pool, drinks that were way too strong, and trashy snacks. The dive bar is where you end your night—where you long for greasy, saucy bites and nostalgic drinks like the vodka cran you bought with your fake ID or the fishbowl you shared with your best friends. Follow this menu to re-create this nostalgic magic.

Another Round!

Yuengling
Premium Beer
America's Oldest Brewers
PENTAX
VOS

SHOOT THE PICKLE

Tajín and dill pickle juice, for rimming the glass

1 ounce vodka

1 ounce dill pickle juice

Small pinch of celery salt

2 dashes Tabasco sauce or your favorite hot sauce

Whole pickle or slice, for garnish

SERVES 1

If you love an extra-dirty martini or a michelada, be sure to try this briny shot. Made with ice-cold pickle juice, vodka, a little celery salt, and hot sauce, this salty, zippy sip is a surprising palate cleanser between drinks and is smoother than you think it will taste. This is *the* shot for savory beverage lovers.

Pour a thin layer of Tajín onto a flat saucer. Dampen the outside rim of a shot glass with pickle juice, then holding the glass at an angle almost parallel to the saucer, roll the dampened edge in the Tajín to coat lightly. Set the glass aside.

In a cocktail shaker, combine the vodka, pickle juice, celery salt, and Tabasco sauce. Add 2 scoops of ice, cover the shaker, and shake hard for 10 to 15 seconds, or until the outside of the shaker is frosty cold to the touch.

Strain into the Tajín-rimmed glass and garnish with the pickle.

ELIZABETH'S TIP

You can use pickle juice from a jar of Vlasic original dills for a signature taste or from Grillo's refrigerated pickles for a mellow garlic flavor. Both are tasty.

Since
Premium

EEUWENOUDE TRADITIE

LOADED CHEESY ENCHILADA NACHOS

FOR THE CHICKEN

Juice of 1½ limes

1 tablespoon olive oil

2 garlic cloves, minced

One 1-ounce packet favorite taco seasoning

2 tablespoons tomato paste

½ cup chicken broth

4 cups shredded cooked chicken breast (about 1 pound; rotisserie chicken works well)

FOR THE NACHOS

One 11-ounce bag sturdy tortilla chips

One 10-ounce can red enchilada sauce

2 cups shredded cheddar cheese

2 cups shredded Monterey Jack cheese

FOR THE GUACAMOLE

1 avocado, halved, pitted, and peeled

2 tablespoons chopped fresh cilantro

Juice of ½ lime

½ teaspoon garlic powder

¼ teaspoon kosher salt

FOR THE TOPPINGS

Chopped fresh cilantro

Thin jalapeño chile slices

Pico de gallo

Pickled onions

Sour cream

SERVES 4 TO 6

Deliciously saucy and meaty, this top-tier bar snack is the love child of enchiladas and nachos. Sturdy tortilla chips are topped with juicy, richly seasoned shredded chicken, red enchilada sauce, and two kinds of melty cheese and slid into the oven. When the nachos emerge, they are crowned with homemade guac and everyone's favorite toppings, from sour cream and cilantro to pickled onions and jalapeños.

Preheat the oven to 350°F. Line a large sheet pan with parchment paper.

TO PREPARE THE CHICKEN, in a medium Dutch oven or heavy saucepan, combine the lime juice, olive oil, garlic, taco seasoning, tomato paste, and broth and stir until smooth. Add the chicken and stir to coat evenly. Place over medium-low heat and cook, stirring occasionally, for 5 to 6 minutes, or until the chicken has soaked up most of the liquid. Remove from the heat.

TO MAKE THE NACHOS, spread half of the chips on the prepared sheet pan. Layer half of the simmered chicken on top of the chips, drizzle half of the enchilada sauce over the chicken, and then top with half each of the Monterey Jack and cheddar cheeses. Layer the remaining chips over the cheese, then top with the remaining chicken, enchilada sauce, and Jack and cheddar cheeses. Bake for 10 minutes, or until the cheeses are melted and bubbly.

TO MAKE THE GUACAMOLE, while the nachos are baking, in a small bowl and using a fork, mash together the avocado, cilantro, lime juice, garlic powder, and salt until smooth.

Remove the nachos from the oven and top with the guacamole and as many of the suggested toppings as you like. Serve right away.

11
8
16
7

CRISPY BUFFALO CAULIFLOWER

1 small head cauliflower

1½ cups buttermilk

¼ cup cornstarch

½ cup all-purpose flour

2 teaspoons garlic powder

1 teaspoon sweet paprika

2 teaspoons chili powder

¼ teaspoon cayenne pepper

1 teaspoon kosher salt

½ teaspoon freshly ground black pepper

2 cups panko bread crumbs

Olive oil cooking spray, for coating the florets

1 cup store-bought Buffalo sauce, plus more for drizzling

Chopped fresh chives, for garnish

Store-bought ranch or blue cheese dressing, for serving

SERVES 4 TO 6

This appetizer is Erewhon meets dive bar energy. Crunchy, saucy, and eaten with your fingers, these cauliflower bites are the ideal snack to nibble on between sips of a light beer (or kombucha). Inspired by their legendary chicken wing namesake, these yummy florets are equal parts elevated and unbothered.

Preheat the oven to 425°F. Top a large sheet pan with one large or two smaller oven-safe wire racks (or use two smaller sheet pans).

Using a large, sharp knife, cut the cauliflower in half vertically, then cut away the core and any leaves. Cut each half into florets.

In a large bowl, whisk together the buttermilk, cornstarch, flour, garlic powder, paprika, chili powder, cayenne pepper, salt, and black pepper until well mixed and lump-free. Add the cauliflower florets and stir until evenly coated with the batter.

Put the panko into a medium shallow bowl and set it alongside the bowl with the cauliflower. One at a time, dip each cauliflower floret into the panko, coating it evenly, and place on the rack on the sheet pan, spacing the florets so they are not touching one another.

Spray the tops of the florets evenly with olive oil spray. Bake for 20 minutes. Remove from the oven, flip the cauliflower, and spray with olive oil spray on the second side. Continue to bake for 10 minutes, or until the cauliflower is crispy. Remove from the oven.

Add the Buffalo sauce to a large bowl. Gently add the crisped cauliflower to the sauce and toss to coat evenly. Return the florets to the rack on the sheet pan, then slide the pan back into the oven and bake for 5 to 10 minutes, or until glazed.

Transfer the florets to a serving platter and garnish with the chives. Drizzle with a little more Buffalo sauce, if desired. Serve hot with a bowl of ranch dressing alongside for dipping.

MILLER BREWING COMPANY MILWAUKEE
Miller
BREWED
HIGH LIFE
ESTD 1903
The Champagne of Beers
12 FLUID OUNCES (.355 LITERS)

SPAGHETT

One 12-ounce bottle Miller High Life beer, chilled

1 ounce Aperol

½ ounce fresh lemon juice

SERVES 1

I love a dive bar that serves a bucket of beers for twenty bucks. It's probably the most wholesome thing that goes on there. I've taken that party-serving style and swapped the beers for spaghetts. A spaghett is a Miller High Life beer (aka "The Champagne of Beers") with a little Aperol and lemon juice added right to the bottle. I'm not a big beer girl, but this I love.

Open the beer bottle and pour out—or drink—1 to 2 ounces of beer. Pour the Aperol and lemon juice into the bottle and gently swirl the bottle to mix the ingredients.

ELIZABETH'S TIP

You can also make this drink with a different crisp lager, such as Peroni or Stella Artois.

HOUR

DRUNKEN CHEESEBURGER DIP

8 ounces lean ground beef (90/10)

2 tablespoons unsalted butter

½ small green bell pepper, seeded and diced

¼ yellow onion, diced

2 garlic cloves, minced

2 tablespoons all-purpose flour

1½ cups whole milk

1½ teaspoons chili powder

1½ teaspoons ground cumin

1½ teaspoons dried oregano

1 teaspoon sweet paprika

1 teaspoon kosher salt

¾ cup shredded cheddar cheese

¾ cup shredded Monterey Jack cheese

Chopped fresh cilantro and minced jalapeño chile, for garnish

Sturdy tortilla chips, for serving

SERVES 6

If you jumped on the Chili's resurgence (I'm looking at you, my girl Taylor!), you must try this cheesy drunken dip. Hearty and warm, this one-skillet dish makes you feel right at home—the kind of comfort food that is even sweeter shared with others. It has everything you want from a good queso with a rich cheeseburger flair.

In a medium skillet (cast iron works well) over medium heat, cook the ground beef, breaking it up with a wooden spoon or spatula and stirring occasionally, for 3 to 4 minutes, or until browned and cooked through. Using a slotted spoon, transfer the beef to a medium bowl and set aside.

Turn down the heat to medium-low and add the butter. When the butter has melted, add the bell pepper and onion and cook, stirring occasionally, for 4 to 5 minutes, or until the onion is tender and translucent. Add the garlic and cook, stirring occasionally, for 1 to 2 minutes, or until fragrant. Stir in the flour, mixing until a smooth paste forms.

Slowly add the milk while stirring constantly, then continue to stir until the mixture comes to a low simmer. Add the chili powder, cumin, oregano, paprika, and salt and stir to mix well.

Turn off the heat and add both cheeses, a handful at a time, stirring after each addition until completely melted before adding the next handful. Stir in the cooked beef.

Transfer to a shallow serving bowl and garnish with the cilantro and jalapeño. Serve hot with tortilla chips.

VODKA CRAN TILL DEATH DO US PART

2 ounces vodka

2 ounces unsweetened pure cranberry juice

1 ounce fresh orange juice

½ ounce fresh lime juice

2 to 3 ounces lemon-lime soda, such as Sprite

Lime wedge, for garnish

SERVES 1

Whenever I hear the words *vodka cran*, I'm immediately transported to a small bar in rural Pennsylvania called Mel's. I was drinking a vodka cran in that very spot when I met Jared, and now every time I sip this fruit-forward cocktail, it reminds me of the summer of 2013 when we met and shared our first kiss in the back of that wonderful little bar (sappy, I know). This drink is similar and nostalgic like the classic but more refined. Pair it with Loaded Cheesy Enchilada Nachos (page 239) for a match made in heaven.

In a cocktail shaker, combine the vodka, cranberry juice, orange juice, and lime juice. Add 2 scoops of ice, cover the shaker, and shake hard for 10 to 15 seconds, or until the outside of the shaker is frosty cold to the touch.

Strain into a collins glass over ice. Top with the lemon-lime soda and stir gently. Garnish with the lime wedge.

DIT IS UW BIER

CHAMPAGNE

INDEX

N

O

P

ACKNOWLEDGMENTS

My community, thank you for every comment, every recipe review. I am so grateful to everyone who cheered me on during good times and bad and who bought *Everyday Entertaining*. You have made this career more fulfilling than I could have ever dreamed. Thank you for giving me a seat at your tables. My friends and family, thank you for being the heartbeat behind these pages. Every dinner party, happy hour, and gathering is made better with you.

My partner and confidant, Jared Storb. You are my first call, my kiss good night, and the steady hand beside me through life's ups and downs. Thank you for always helping me with the dishes, falling asleep on the couch next to me during late-night writing sessions, supporting me while I got back on my feet after my mom passed away, and for cheering me on as I wrote this book. It has not been easy, but I'm glad you (and Rascal) were by my side. I love you so hard.

To my mom, even though I won't be able to hand this book to you, you live in the pages. Your hosting style, details, and thoughtfulness shine through everything I make. I wish I could have brought you the first copy of the book and watched your eyes glisten. I miss you beyond words, and I love you so very much.

Dad, it has not been an easy couple of years, but we made it. I am so grateful to have you here. Thank you for always supporting my crazy dreams with words of encouragement and for every time you asked how the book was coming along. I appreciate all that you've done in life and I love you.

My grandparents! Nanna Jane and Norval, Pappa and Nanna Pam—I'm a lucky girl to have you all in my life. Your wisdom, humor, guidance, and friendship are so important to me. Every moment we spend together is one I cherish. Pappa, thank you *so* much for being my butter star. Doing that photoshoot with you is something I'll treasure forever, and I promise you'll see some royalties, okay?

Ralph, I'm so grateful we have each other. Through life's challenges and celebrations, you've always been a source of laughter, love, and support. I also love making you a fun sister treat. Kisses!

TO MY TEAM

First, I have to brag a little about my A+ team. Every recipe, photograph, design choice, food styling, prop styling, and even wardrobe styling were brought to life by an incredible team of women. With your help, we created something truly magical. Thank you for your tenacity, hard work, and creativity. This book is as much yours as it is mine.

Abagail, thank you for your beautiful design work, incredible photography, and creative vision. From the beginning, your talent helped shape the look and feel of this book in ways I never would have thought possible.

Isabella, thank you for approaching every recipe and styling with care, precision, and curiosity. You provide a truly scientific je ne sais quoi. Thank you for pushing me to test something ten times and for your insights into how to make everything absolutely perfect and beautiful.

Payton, thank you for jumping into this project with enthusiasm and creativity. Your eye for style, both in food and fashion, helped bring this world to life.

TO MY GIRLS

Alex, my best friend for decades and my muse. Thank you for showing up, modeling, encouraging me, and inspiring so many of the moments captured in these pages. Your friendship has been one of the greatest gifts of my life.

Sierra, thank you for being the first person I send nearly everything to. Your perspective, taste, honesty, and encouragement have guided me through countless decisions. I am endlessly grateful for your friendship and support.

Adesha and Taylor, some of my absolute best happy hour memories are with you two. Thank you for your friendship, honesty, laughter, and all of the inspiration you bring to my life.

Luke, thank you for your enthusiasm and support and for your kindness to Mr. Rascal. Bringing the mojitos to life could only be done with you. Cheers!

Amy, there are not enough words to express how grateful I am to you. Creating another book together has been one of the greatest joys of my career. You are far more than an editor. You are a trusted guide, a wealth of knowledge, and a constant source of encouragement. Your talent, expertise, and belief in this project made it better at every stage. I light up every time I receive an email from you. Thank you for bringing this world to life with me.

Edward and everyone at Weldon Owen, thank you for believing in this project from the beginning. Your trust, guidance, and support helped transform a dream into a reality.

weldon**owen**
an imprint of Insight Editions
P.O. Box 3088
San Rafael, CA 94912
www.weldonowen.com

CEO Raoul Goff
SVP Group Publisher Jeff McLaughlin
VP Publisher Roger Shaw
Associate Publisher Thom O'Hearn
Executive Editor Edward Ash-Milby
Assistant Editor Kayla Belser
Production Editor Ivy Long
Art Director Megan Sinead Bingham
Production Designer Jean Hwang
VP Manufacturing Alix Nicholaeff
Production Manager Deena Hashem
Strategic Production Planner Lina s Palma-Temena

Project Editor Amy Marr
Photographers Abagail Halstead and Elizabeth Van Lierde
Designer Abagail Halstead
Food Stylists Isabella Parham, Abagail Halstead, and Elizabeth Van Lierde
Recipe Testers Isabella Parham and Payton King
Wardrobe Stylist Payton King

Weldon Owen would also like to thank Sharon Silva and Ellen Foreman.

ISBN: 979-8-88674-421-7
Manufactured in China by Insight Editions
10 9 8 7 6 5 4 3 2 1

ROOTS of PEACE REPLANTED PAPER

Insight Editions, in association with Roots of Peace, will plant two trees for each tree used in the manufacturing of this book. Roots of Peace is an internationally renowned humanitarian organization dedicated to eradicating land mines worldwide and converting war-torn lands into productive farms and wildlife habitats. Roots of Peace will plant two million fruit and nut trees in Afghanistan and provide farmers there with the skills and support necessary for sustainable land use.